Access
My eLab

SAY WHAT YOU MEAN ②

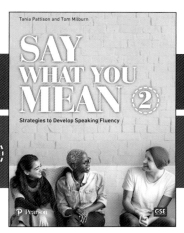

Tania Pattison and Tom Milburn

SAY WHAT YOU MEAN ②

Strategies to Develop Speaking Fluency

P Pearson   GSE

TO REGISTER

D1616274

❶ Go to **mybookshelf.pearsonerpi.com**

❷ Follow the instructions. When asked for your access code, please type the code provided underneath the blue sticker.

❸ To access **My eLab** at any time, go to http://mybookshelf.pearsonerpi.com. **Bookmark this page for quicker access.**

Access to My eLab is valid for 12 months from the date of registration.

WARNING! This book CANNOT BE RETURNED if the access code has been uncovered.

Note: Once you have registered, you will need to join your online class. Ask your teacher to provide you with the class ID.

TEACHER Access Code

To obtain an access code for My eLab, please contact your Pearson ELT consultant.

1 800 263-3678, ext. 2
pearsonerpi.com/help

W139540 (A39541)

3849

Tania Pattison and Tom Milburn

SAY WHAT YOU MEAN ②

Strategies to Develop Speaking Fluency

Product Owner
Stephan Leduc

Managing Editor
Sharnee Chait

Project Editor
Jennifer McAliney

Proofreader
Paula Sarson

Rights and Permissions Coordinator
Aude Maggiori

Text Rights and Permissions
Rachel Irwin

Art Director
Hélène Cousineau

Graphic Design Manager
Estelle Cuillerier

Book and Cover Design
Andrée Lauzon

Book Layout
Talisman illustration design

Cover Photo
Shutterstock © Rawpixel.com

The publisher wishes to thank the following people for their helpful comments and suggestions:

Randy Berry, Seneca College

Anita Chaudhuri, Mount Royal University

Janine DeForge, CultureWorks ESL Inc.

Nathaniel Hautecoeur, English Montreal School Board

Vasie Kelos, Seneca College

Alayna Lamoureux, Vancouver International College

Stephanie Lapointe, Université du Québec à Chicoutimi

Karen McCoubrey, Cégep de Sainte-Foy

James Papple, Brock University

Ana-Marija Petrunic, University of Calgary

Cyndy Reimer, Douglas College

Debra Robinson, Centennial College

Tayebeh Shalmani, Columbia College

© ÉDITIONS DU RENOUVEAU PÉDAGOGIQUE INC. (ERPI), 2019
ERPI publishes and distributes PEARSON ELT products in Canada.

1611 Crémazie Boulevard East, 10th Floor
Montréal, Québec H2M 2P2
Canada
Telephone : 1 800 263-3678
Fax: 514 334-4720
information@pearsonerpi.com
pearsonerpi.com

DANGER
PHOTOCOPYING
KILLS BOOKS

All rights reserved.
No part of this publication may be reproduced, stored in a retrieval system, or transmitted in any form or by any means, electronic, mechanical, photocopying, recording, or otherwise without the prior written permission of ÉDITIONS DU RENOUVEAU PÉDAGOGIQUE INC.

Registration of copyright—Bibliothèque et Archives nationales du Québec, 2019
Registration of copyright—Library and Archives Canada, 2019

Printed in Canada

ISBN 978-2-7613-9540-3   1234567890 HLN 23 22 21 20 19
(82021428)   139540 ABCD   OF10

INTRODUCTION

Say What You Mean 2 is intended to develop and consolidate speaking skills in students at the CEFR B1 level who intend to use English for general purposes, academic study, or for the workplace.

The book presents language that will be useful to students whose personal, academic, and professional needs include discussion skills, presentation skills, and group work. Students learn and practise phrases and expressions that they can use to share their opinions, deliver information, reach a consensus, keep a discussion on track, and much more.

Language development, however, is not the only focus of the book. An important feature of the book is the focus on strategies for successful communication. Students taking part in discussions need to know more than language to agree and disagree: they need to find ways to develop confidence in speaking, continue a discussion that appears to have run its course, and address issues such as classmates who are hard to understand or who do not wish to contribute. Students planning presentations need strategies for designing effective slides and overcoming nerves. Those whose academic or professional needs include working in teams need an understanding of how groups function and how to work successfully with others. Those who need to find solutions to problems may wonder how to come up with creative ideas. The book provides tips in all of these areas, and other situations as well.

To meet these objectives, the book presents a variety of topics of current and general interest; these include social media, sports, fashion, technology, housing, and more. Each unit starts with either a reading or a listening task; the latter is based on authentic news stories from media sources. The texts were chosen for their ability to stimulate discussion and critical thinking. Students complete a variety of pair, group, and whole-class tasks, from responses to situations to problem-solving activities to poster presentations to debates. Vocabulary development is included in each unit. A final Go Further activity at the end of each unit allows students to use online resources to investigate a real-life person or situation related to the theme of the unit.

Effective communication is vital to success in everyday life, academia, and in the workplace. *Say What You Mean 2* allows students to build on the skills they already have to become effective and convincing speakers in a variety of situations.

ACKNOWLEDGEMENTS

Many people have provided support and encouragement at various stages of writing this book. We especially appreciate colleagues who have provided feedback at various stages. The authors want to acknowledge the Pearson team, especially Stephan Leduc for his enthusiasm for the project, and our editor Sharnee Chait for her guidance.

Tania Pattison and Tom Milburn
Peterborough, Canada

HIGHLIGHTS

The first page outlines the **learning objectives** in the unit.

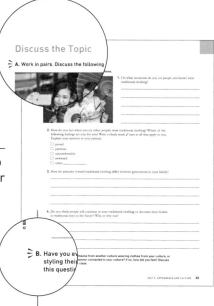

Discuss the Topic allows you to discuss the unit topic using your prior knowledge.

This shows that you are involved in a **speaking task**.

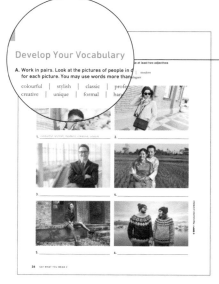

Develop Your Vocabulary helps your comprehension by introducing vocabulary connected to the topic of the unit.

Build Your Knowledge introduces a reading or a video to provide context for the unit topic. There are six videos and six readings in the book.

Before activities help you reflect on the topic.

After activities focus on comprehension.

Share Your Ideas provides guided questions to help you think critically about the reading or video and to discuss issues.

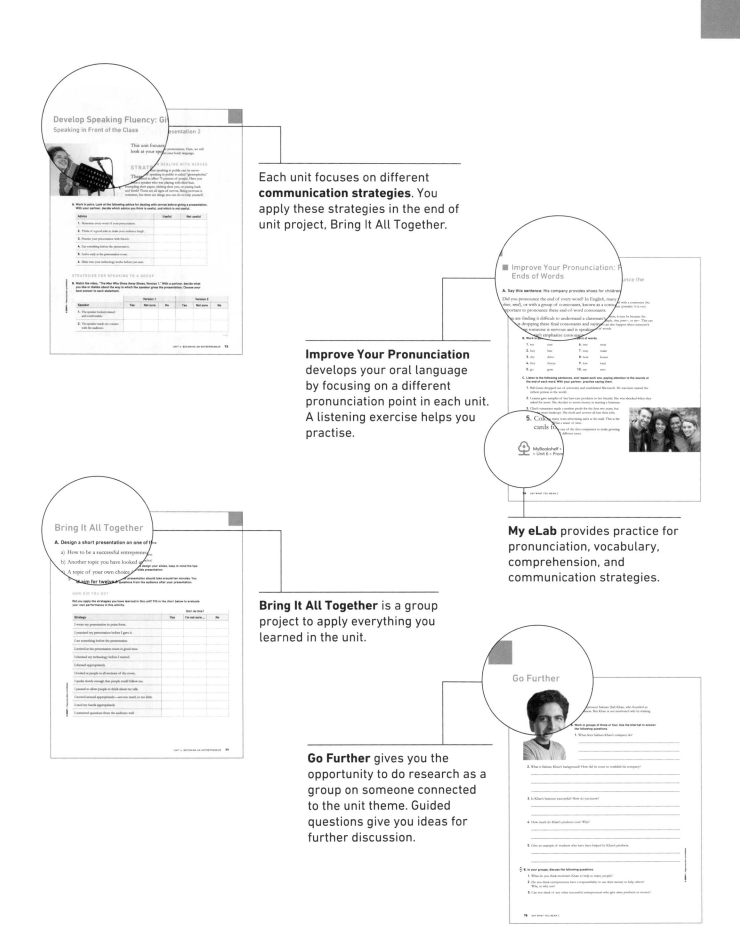

Each unit focuses on different **communication strategies**. You apply these strategies in the end of unit project, Bring It All Together.

Improve Your Pronunciation develops your oral language by focusing on a different pronunciation point in each unit. A listening exercise helps you practise.

My eLab provides practice for pronunciation, vocabulary, comprehension, and communication strategies.

Bring It All Together is a group project to apply everything you learned in the unit.

Go Further gives you the opportunity to do research as a group on someone connected to the unit theme. Guided questions give you ideas for further discussion.

SCOPE AND SEQUENCE FOR COURSEBOOK AND MY ELAB

UNIT	SPEAKING	CRITICAL THINKING	VOCABULARY	PRONUNCIATION
UNIT 1 **FAMILIES AND** **SOCIAL MEDIA**	• Develop confidence when speaking in a group • Express your opinion on topics of current interest • Ask people about their opinions	• Think critically about social media and families	• Explore meaning in words related to social media and family	• Understand which words are stressed in a sentence
UNIT 2 **ETHICS** **IN SPORTS**	• Agree with someone's opinion • Politely disagree with someone's opinion	• Think critically about ethics in sports	• Explore meaning in words related to ethics in sports	• Understand how stress changes the meaning of a sentence
UNIT 3 **APPEARANCE** **AND CULTURE**	• Keep a conversation going	• Think critically about appearance and culture	• Explore meaning in words related to clothing	• Distinguish between the /r/ and /l/ sounds
UNIT 4 **OLD TECH,** **NEW TECH**	• Deal with challenging situations in group discussions • Talk to group members in challenging situations	• Think critically about current technology applications	• Explore meaning in words related to technology	• Use intonation to identify whether or not a speaker is finished
UNIT 5 **LIVING SMALL**	• Plan a presentation • Design effective slides • Give a short presentation on the topic of homes	• Think critically about small homes	• Explore meaning in words related to small homes	• Distinguish between the voiced /ð/ and voiceless /θ/ *th* sounds
UNIT 6 **BECOMING AN** **ENTREPRENEUR**	• Develop skills in delivering a presentation • Give a short presentation to your class	• Think critically about starting and running a business	• Explore meaning in words related to entrepreneurship	• Pronounce the ends of words

UNIT	SPEAKING	CRITICAL THINKING	VOCABULARY	PRONUNCIATION
UNIT 7 **TRAVEL AND** **CUSTOMS**	• Learn about the dynamics of groups • Learn strategies to develop collaboration skills • Take part in a group problem-solving activity	• Think critically about differences between customs in different cultures	• Explore meaning in words related to travel and customs	• Link words together
UNIT 8 **URBAN GREEN** **SPACES**	• Learn about the importance of creativity • Learn strategies to develop creativity • Take part in a group activity requiring creative thought	• Think critically about the impact of green space	• Explore meaning in words related to environmental concerns	• Distinguish between the /iː/ and /ɪ/ sounds
UNIT 9 **ALL IN A** **DAY'S WORK**	• Learn to design an effective poster • Work in a group to find a solution to a problem • Present your ideas in the form of a poster presentation	• Think critically about issues in the workplace	• Explore meaning in words related to feelings about work	• Use reduced speech to make your speech more fluent
UNIT 10 **IT'S THE LAW**	• Learn to take part in whole-class discussions • Discuss a controversial topic with your class	• Think critically about issues related to crime	• Explore meaning in words related to crime	• Understand the use of the /ə/ sound
UNIT 11 **ONLINE GAMES**	• Develop strategies for speaking persuasively • Take part in a debate	• Think critically about issues related to playing games online	• Explore meaning in words related to playing games online	• Use appropriate stress for compound nouns
UNIT 12 **ON THE SCREEN**	• Practise taking part in whole-class discussions • Lead a discussion with your class • Review strategies	• Think critically about issues related to movies	• Explore meaning in words related to movies	• Address individual pronunciation challenges

TABLE OF CONTENTS

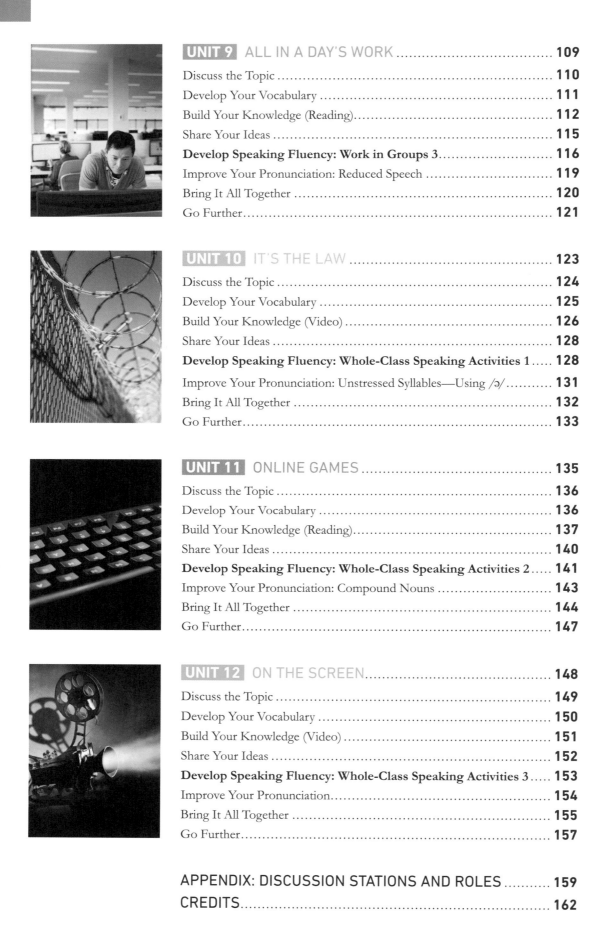

In this unit, you will learn to do the following:

Think critically about social media and families.

Use vocabulary related to social media and communication.

Develop confidence when speaking in a group.

Express your opinion on topics of current interest.

Ask other people about their opinions.

Understand which words are stressed in a sentence.

FAMILIES AND SOCIAL MEDIA

Discuss the Topic

A. **A. Work in pairs. Discuss the following questions.**

1. Which of the following social media sites do you use? Check all that you are a member of.

   ☐ Facebook   ☐ Instagram   ☐ Snapchat   ☐ Reddit

   ☐ Twitter   ☐ Tumblr   ☐ LinkedIn   ☐ other _____

2. How much time do you spend every day on social media?

   _____

3. What do you use social media for? To chat, to learn, or for other reasons?

   _____

4. Which social media sites do you think are useful? Which are less useful? Why?

   _____

5. How many people are you connected with on social media? Are any of them your family members?

   _____

B. Should young adults be friends with their parents on social media? Discuss this question with your class.

Develop Your Vocabulary

A. Work in pairs. Choose the best phrase to complete each of the following sentences.

keep an eye on | keep in touch with | check up on | get along well with | get in touch with

1. I am 20 years old. My mom and dad don't need to _____ me all the time. I'm not a child. I can make my own choices.

2. Social media is a good way to _____ someone in an emergency, or to make plans for the weekend.

3. I go to college in another city. My parents use social media to _____ me, to make sure I'm safe.

4. Do you _____ your parents, or do you find it difficult to communicate with them?

5. When you go to live in a new country, it is important to _____ your friends from home. Don't forget about them!

© ERPI • Reproduction prohibited

B. With your partner, match each word with its meaning.

Words		Meanings
1. post (verb)		**a)** name someone on social media
2. network (noun)		**b)** write on social media
3. status (noun)		**c)** put a photo or document on social media
4. tag (verb)		**d)** people you are connected with on social media
5. upload (verb)		**e)** your current situation; what you're doing

C. Tell your partner about the following:

1. How your parents check up on you (or, if you have children, how you check up on them).

2. A family member you get along well with.

3. Someone you have kept in touch with for a long time.

4. The most recent thing you posted on social media.

5. Something you have uploaded recently.

6. A time you were tagged by someone.

MyBookshelf > My eLab > Exercises
> Unit 1 > Vocabulary

Build Your Knowledge

BEFORE YOU READ

This is Julia, nineteen. She is a university student who has moved away from home to go to university. Her parents now want to connect with Julia on social media. Should she accept?

A. Work in pairs. With your partner, list three reasons why Julia should be friends on social media with her parents.

1. _____

2. _____

3. _____

B. Now list three reasons why this might not be a good idea.

1. _____

2. _____

3. _____

C. Work in pairs. Should parents be connected with their adult children on social media? Read six young people's opinions on this question.

D. After you read each person's statement, write the person's name in the chart. The first is done for you.

I think it's fine to be friends with Mom and Dad on social media.	I don't know. I can see both sides of the argument.	I don't want to be friends with my parents on social media.
		Edward

Edward, 20

I hate the thought of my parents following me on social media. I like to post what I think about the world, what I'm doing with my friends, pictures of nights out, and socializing. I don't want my mom and dad checking up on me all the time. My parents are from a different generation, and they just make negative comments about what I do with my time, how I dress, the music I listen to, and what my friends are like. It's none of their business! They don't accept that I am an adult and that I have my own life now.

Diana, 22

I used to dislike my parents seeing my social media posts, but I have a different attitude about it now. I understand that they like to know what I'm doing in my life. Also, they can get in touch with me in an emergency. I don't post anything that might upset them. I just post really normal material. They like to "like" my pictures and make comments, and why shouldn't they? They're my mother and father, and they know what's going on in my life. I have no problem with it.

Chad, 18

My mom heard all of her friends talking about being on social media, so she asked me to help her get started. She doesn't have much experience with computers, and she didn't have the skills to set up her own account, so I showed her how to do it. But then she said she wanted to be part of my network. I think she wants to keep an eye on me. I don't have anything to hide, but I really don't want my mom to see everything I post. I love my parents, and I feel really guilty that I don't want to be friends with my mom online! I'm not sure what to do!

Millie, 20

I get along well with my mom and dad, but they are very traditional, and they have firm ideas about what kind of lifestyle I should have. I have different ideas, but I also respect them. So I have two different social media accounts. I use one with my actual name where I post basic information, especially a lot of family photographs and good marks in school. Then I have another account with just my first name, and my friends know that's where I post more fun things like parties. I would never want my parents to see my "real" account.

© **ERPI** • Reproduction prohibited

Russell, 23

Last year I went backpacking in Europe for the summer. I realized that being on social media with my family was actually a good idea. My parents wanted to know where I was travelling and what I was doing, and it made more sense for me to post about my travels on social media so it was easy to keep in touch with them all the time. Sure, they might have seen a few embarrassing pictures, but the advantage was that they knew where I was all the time. Besides, my parents are quite modern; they are not easily upset by what I post.

Wendy, 25

The most embarrassing experience of my entire life happened because of social media! I told my parents I couldn't go to a family dinner because I had to study for an exam. The truth is, I wanted to go to a party with some friends. I didn't realize some of my friends were taking pictures and then posting them on social media, and tagging me by name. My dad follows me, and he saw the pictures! As you can imagine, my parents weren't very happy about how I had lied to them. I never want to be in that situation again.

AFTER YOU READ

E. Now, with your partner, decide whose parent is responding to each of the statements above. Use each name only once.

Edward | Diana | Chad | Millie | Russell | Wendy

1. I was very disappointed by _____'s behaviour, but I understand what happened. Young people need to be more careful with social media.

2. I wish _____ would trust us. We don't want to be controlling parents. We just want to keep in touch.

3. _____ likes to travel, and naturally, we worry about safety in other parts of the world. Social media is very helpful to us because we know he's okay and we can relax.

4. _____ is young, and young people sometimes make bad choices. We want to help our children to make the right decisions about who they spend time with.

5. Things were very different when we were young. Fortunately, _____ shares our values and is doing very well. We are proud parents!

6. _____ is an adult, not a child. We have a good relationship with all our adult children because we trust them. Trust is very important.

MyBookshelf > My eLab > Exercises
> Unit 1 > Parents and Social Media

© **ERPI** • Reproduction prohibited

Share Your Ideas

Join another pair to make a group of four. With your group, discuss the following questions.

1. Look again at the six young people you met in Build Your Knowledge. Which person's opinion or experience is closest to your own?

2. What do you like and dislike about different forms of social media? Why do you think some are more popular with younger or older people?

3. Which of the following have happened to you? Share your experiences.
   a) Have you ever posted something online and felt bad about it later?
   b) Have you ever seen something posted online by a friend and felt angry about it?
   c) Have you ever refused to be connected with someone on social media? Why?

4. Read the following statement from a parent. What would you say to this parent?

> We miss our little girl so much now that she's away from home! We just want to keep in touch with her and make sure she's happy. We've always been so close since she was a child. We want to make sure we know when she's upset and needs support, but we also want to find out all the great things that are happening to her. We especially want to make sure we keep up with what she's doing at university in case she needs any help. Social media is such a great thing—no one has to worry about writing emails or making phone calls!

5. Do you take any steps to make sure you are safe on social media? If so, what are they?

Develop Speaking Fluency: Take Part in a Discussion 1
Express Your Opinion

If you are planning to study at university or college in an English-speaking country, you will need to take part in group discussions. It is not enough to learn information, memorize it, and repeat it on an exam. You will need to think carefully about what you have learned, and you will need to express your thoughts about it. There is often no "correct" answer.

STRATEGIES FOR BUILDING CONFIDENCE

Are you nervous about speaking in front of other students? Many students are. They are afraid their classmates won't understand them or might laugh at them. If you are a less-confident speaker, there are some strategies you can follow to build your confidence.

A. Work in pairs. Look at the following strategies to build your confidence. Decide whether you should or shouldn't do each one. Underline *Do* or *Don't* at the beginning of each sentence. Then, choose the best reason for your answer. One reason is extra.

© ERPI • Reproduction prohibited

Strategy		Reason
1. Do | <u>Don't</u> wait a few weeks before speaking, so that you can become comfortable in the class.	c	**a)** No one will judge your use of language. Your classmates will be worrying about their own English, not yours.
2. Do | Don't be a good listener.		**b)** No one will notice if you make a grammar mistake. The important thing is to make your opinion clear.
3. Do | Don't plan in your head exactly what you are going to say before you speak.		**c)** The longer you wait to start speaking, the harder it will become. Don't wait until you feel confident; speaking will *make* you feel confident.
4. Do | Don't be afraid to express an opinion that is different from other people's opinions.		**d)** If you ask someone to repeat, your classmates will think your English is weak.
5. Do | Don't worry about having perfect grammar.		**e)** Everyone's opinion is good. There are often no "right" or "wrong" answers in group discussions.
6. Do | Don't speak slowly.		**f)** If you aren't sure about something, there is a good chance your classmates will also not have understood.
7. Do | Don't ask if you don't understand what someone is saying.		**g)** You don't have time to do this; discussions move too quickly.
8. Do | Don't worry about what other people think about your English.		**h)** People often speak too fast when they are nervous. Your listeners need time to think about what you are saying.
		i) You will learn from the opinions of others. Show that you are listening (nod or smile), and don't interrupt.

STRATEGIES FOR EXPRESSING YOUR OPINION

B. Work in pairs. Read the following conversation. Then, find TWO ways the speakers do each of the following:

a) express positive opinions

b) express negative opinions

c) say that they are not sure

d) ask others what they think

Edward: So, Chad, are you ready for your big trip?

Chad: I am, but I can't believe this! Edward, my parents want to follow me on Instagram! I don't want them to see everything I'm doing.

Diana: Is that really so bad? I think it's the best way to keep in touch with them while you are travelling.

Chad: I think it's a really bad idea, Diana! They're going to worry about me if I post photos or write about stuff they think is dangerous.

© ERPI • Reproduction prohibited

Wendy: I can see it both ways. It's easier for you to let them follow you, so you don't have to worry about getting in touch with them every day. But you shouldn't be afraid of posting photos.

Russell: I like the idea of your parents following you on social media. When I was travelling overseas, my parents wanted me to email them every night! Sometimes it was hard to find Wi-Fi, and other times I was busy.

Edward: You know, it's not just your trip. How do you feel about them following you when you come back home?

Chad: Well, I finally have my own life, and my parents treat me like an adult. I don't think it's a good idea.

Russell: I think it's a great idea to be on social media with my parents. Maybe it sounds mean, but when they can see what I post, I don't have to get in touch so often. It's easier for me!

Millie: I have mixed feelings about it. I have two different accounts, one for my family and one for my friends. Sometimes it's hard to remember which is which, and how to keep it all straight.

Diana: So what do you think, Chad? What are you going to do?

Ways to express a positive opinion

1. _____

2. _____

Ways to express a negative opinion

1. _____

2. _____

Ways to show that you're not sure

1. _____

2. _____

Ways to ask about someone's opinion

1. _____

2. _____

MyBookshelf > My eLab > Exercises
> Unit 1 > Strategies

■ Improve Your Pronunciation: Which Word to Stress 1

A. Say this sentence: I finally have my own life, and my parents treat me like an adult.

In English, not every word has equal stress. Some words are more heavily stressed than others.

Which word(s) did you stress in the sentence above? Did you stress *finally, have, own, life, parents, treat,* and *adult*? These are content words. **Content words** are nouns, verbs, adjectives, and adverbs. They give meaning to the sentence, and they are usually stressed.

Function words, such as pronouns, conjunctions, prepositions, articles, and auxiliary verbs provide the grammar for the sentence. They are not usually stressed, except for emphasis.

B. Work in pairs. Practise saying the following sentences. Underline the words that you stressed.

1. I hate the thought of my parents following me on social media.

2. My parents are from a different generation.

© ERPI • Reproduction prohibited

3. I think she wants to keep an eye on me.

4. What do you think about getting an Instagram account?

5. We kept in touch by email when I was travelling overseas.

6. My parents can reach me quickly in an emergency.

7. Diana has over three thousand people in her online network.

8. I have mixed feelings about this question.

C. Listen to check your answers. Repeat the sentences you hear.

MyBookshelf > My eLab > Exercises
> Unit 1 > Pronunciation

Bring It All Together

A. The following people have sent messages to their friends asking for advice. You are going to help them to solve their problems. On your own, read each message, and decide what advice you would give. Make notes in the space beside each problem.

> My mom has just learned how to upload photos. She keeps putting photographs of me on social media, and these are really embarrassing. I'm talking about baby pictures where I have baby food all over my face, or pictures of me in awful clothes from ten years ago. She always tags me, so my friends have seen these pictures, and they keep laughing at me. I've asked my mom to stop, but she thinks these photos are cute. What should I do?

Laura, 23

_____
_____
_____
_____
_____
_____
_____
_____

> I'm away from home at university. My dad sent my girlfriend a contact request, and she accepted. Big mistake! He then got in touch with her to tell her that I have important exams coming up, and she needs to spend less time with me. Of course, she's very upset. I've told my dad I'm angry, I'm doing really well in my classes, and I won't let him down. He just says I'll be grateful to him when I'm a successful doctor. Please help me!

Harry, 21

_____
_____
_____
_____
_____
_____
_____
_____

© ERPI • Reproduction prohibited

I get along well with my mom, and we're friends on social media. Every time I post a picture or a status update, she calls me. If I'm playing sports outside, she worries that I'm going to catch a cold. If I'm wearing a short skirt, she thinks I'm not dressed warmly enough. If I eat fast food, she writes that I need to eat better. I know she loves me and cares about me, and I don't want to hurt her feelings, but she's driving me crazy! Any advice?

Gabriella, 19

B. Now work in pairs. Share your thoughts with your partner, and find out about your partner's opinions. Discuss your reasons for your opinions. Do you agree?

C. Join another pair and share your opinions. In groups of four, try to reach a decision on what advice you will give to Laura, Harry, and Gabriella.

USEFUL PHRASES

Express a positive opinion
I think it's a great idea.
I like the idea of ...

Express a negative opinion
I think it's a really bad idea.
I don't think it's a good idea.

Show that you're not sure
I have mixed feelings about ...
I can see it both ways.

Ask about someone's opinion
What do you think?
How do you feel about ...?

HOW DID YOU DO?

Did you apply the strategies you have learned in this unit? Fill in the chart below to evaluate your own performance in this activity.

Strategy	Did I do this?		
	Yes	I'm not sure ...	No
I listened carefully to other students' opinions.			
I spoke naturally; I didn't plan my sentences in advance.			
I wasn't afraid to express opinions that were different.			
I didn't worry too much about small grammar mistakes.			
I spoke slowly enough.			

© **ERPI** • Reproduction prohibited

Strategy	Did I do this?		
	Yes	I'm not sure ...	No
I asked someone to repeat if I didn't understand them.			
I used suitable language to express my opinions.			
I used suitable language to ask others what they thought.			

Go Further

In 2012, an American student called Aubrey Ireland said her parents made her feel like a dog who was wearing a collar. A judge in a law court ordered Aubrey's parents, David and Julie, to have no contact with her.

A. Work in groups of three or four. Use the Internet to answer the following questions.

1. How old was Aubrey when this happened? Where and what was she studying?

_____

_____

2. What did Aubrey's parents do to her computer?

_____

3. In what other ways did they try to control her life?

_____

4. How did Aubrey's parents explain their behaviour?

_____

5. What happened when Aubrey's parents stopped paying her university tuition fees?

_____

B. In your groups, discuss the following questions.

1. Aubrey's parents were paying for her education. Does that give them a good reason to follow her activities? Why, or why not?

2. What do you think Aubrey's relationship with her parents is like today?

3. What would you have done in Aubrey's situation?

UNIT 2

Think critically about topics related to ethics in sports.

Use vocabulary related to sports and ethics.

Agree with someone's opinion.

Politely disagree with someone's opinion.

Understand how stress changes the meaning of a sentence.

ETHICS IN SPORTS

Discuss the Topic

A. Work in pairs. Look at the following examples of unethical behaviour in sports. Guess the correct sport for each situation.

1. During the 1986 World Cup, Argentinian player Diego Maradona used his hand to score an important goal in a match against England. The referee did not notice, but video later showed what had happened. Argentina won the match 2–1 and went on to win the tournament. Maradona admits that with today's technology, his goal would not be allowed.

    Sport: _____

2. Rosie Ruiz was the women's winner of the 1980 Boston Marathon, with a time of 2:31:56. However, it turned out that she had not run the entire race. Instead, she had jumped onto the course shortly before the finish line. It emerged that earlier, in the New York Marathon, she had taken the subway to the end of the race.

    Sport: _____

3. At the 1976 Olympics in Montreal, Boris Onischenko wired his sword so it would trigger the electronic scoring system and register a hit against his opponent. This gave him points he had not earned. He was caught when his opponents suspected he was cheating and complained. He was disqualified and was sent home in disgrace.

    Sport: _____

4. In the mid-1990s, Michelle Smith from Ireland held records in freestyle, breaststroke, and butterfly events and won four Olympic medals. Her coach, who was also her husband, was a known drug user. In 1998, a drugs test found whiskey in Michelle's urine. Had she added the whiskey to hide the presence of drugs? She was banned from competing for four years.

    Sport: _____

5. In 1919, eight members of the Chicago White Sox took various sums of money in return for "throwing" (losing on purpose) the 1919 World Series. The Series was won by the Cincinnati Reds. The eight players were banned for life and never played professionally again.

    Sport: _____

6. In 1994, Nancy Kerrigan finished a practice session on the ice and was attacked as she walked to her changing room. She was hit on the knee with a hard bat. The attacker had been hired by the ex-husband of her rival, Tonya Harding. Kerrigan recovered from her injury and won an Olympic silver medal. Harding became a professional boxer several years later.

    Sport: _____

7. In some sports, the top female performers are very young. Dong Fangxiao helped her team win bronze medals at the 1999 World Championships and the 2000 Olympics. However, it later emerged that she had given a false date of birth. She had been only thirteen in 1999 and fourteen in 2000, so had been too young to compete legally. The Chinese team lost its medals in both events.

    Sport: _____

© **ERPI** • Reproduction prohibited

© ERPI • Reproduction prohibited

B. Which do you think are the three worst cases of cheating? Discuss this question with your class.

1. _____

2. _____

3. _____

Develop Your Vocabulary

A. Work in pairs. Choose the best word to complete each of the following sentences.

1. The team's _____ told them they had to work harder than ever to win their next game.

   a) referee

   b) coach

2. The weightlifter was _____ from all future competitions after testing positive for drug use.

   a) banned

   b) disqualified

3. The Kings' chief _____ for many years has been the Hawks; there is a long history of competition between the two teams.

   a) rival

   b) sponsor

4. The runner was _____ after he started the race too early twice in a row.

   a) unethical

   b) disqualified

5. The boxer knocked his _____ to the mat as the fight was coming to an end.

   a) opponent

   b) sponsor

6. It is _____ for trainers to encourage their players to cheat.

   a) unethical

   b) disqualified

7. Ten teams took part in the first _____ of the soccer season.

   a) rival

   b) tournament

8. The spectators were angry when the _____ gave the star player a red card.

   a) opponent

   b) referee

9. A fast-food restaurant is the main _____ of the children's soccer league.
   a) sponsor
   b) rival

10. The Kings' _____ is a gold crown on a white background.
    a) tournament
    b) logo

 **B. Tell your partner about the following:**

1. A sports tournament you have competed in.

2. The best coach you have ever had.

3. The most difficult opponent you have ever faced.

4. Someone who has been your rival.

5. Something you have seen in sports that you think is unethical.

6. A team's logo that you like.

MyBookshelf > My eLab > Exercises
> Unit 2 > Vocabulary

Build Your Knowledge

BEFORE YOU WATCH

A. Discuss these questions with your class.

1. Do you know any sports teams or individual athletes that have a corporate sponsor? Name some.

2. Which sports teams or individual athletes wear uniforms with a corporate logo? Give some examples.

3. What would you do if you played on a team whose business practices conflicted with your own personal beliefs?

VIDEO: TEEN SOCCER PLAYER FACES A MORAL DILEMMA

B. Watch the video. In this video, you will learn about a teenaged girl, Freyja Reed. Freyja's soccer club has a new corporate sponsor—one whose business practices Freyja does not agree with.

© **ERPI** • Reproduction prohibited

C. Work in pairs. Answer these questions.

1. Why was Freyja Reed excited to play soccer in her community?

_____

2. What does the company Marine Harvest do?

_____

3. Why was Freyja's soccer club happy to have this sponsor?

_____

4. Why are Freyja and environmentalists opposed to salmon farming?

_____

5. Freyja's mother says, "I'm really concerned with kids being used as billboards." What does she mean by this?

_____

6. What message was contained in the email sent by the soccer club to Freyja and her mother?

_____

7. What advice does Ian Roberts from Marine Harvest offer to Freyja?

_____

MyBookshelf > My eLab > Exercises
> Unit 2 > Teen Soccer Player

Share Your Ideas

Join another pair to make a group of four. With your group, discuss the following questions.

1. How did this story make you feel about the following?
   a) Freyja
   b) the team
   c) the sponsor

2. What ethical issues are raised by this story?

3. Look at the following responses to the story. Who do you think makes the strongest argument? Who makes the weakest? Why? Rank the statements in order from strong (1) to weak (5).

© ERPI • Reproduction prohibited

Violet: If Freyja doesn't like the sponsor of the team, she doesn't have to play for the team. If she really wants to follow her beliefs, she should find another team whose sponsor she likes.

Josh: Sports teams do not control the opinions of their players. If Freyja's team managers don't like the fact that she spoke to the media, that's their problem. Freyja is entitled to say whatever she wants.

Melissa: Freyja is only fourteeen years old; she can't possibly have such strong opinions. Her mother is using her daughter to share her own beliefs about salmon farming. This is not right.

Felix: Freyja is not much of a team player if she complains on TV about her team. Her first loyalty should be to her team. There is a risk that Marine Harvest will end their sponsorship of the soccer team, and this will hurt Freyja's teammates.

Tamara: Controversial companies like Marine Harvest should not be sponsoring kids' teams. There are other ways to advertise their business without involving children. It is unethical to treat children in this way. Freyja's mom is absolutely correct.

4. After this story became public, it was announced that Freyja would no longer be playing for her soccer team. She was left with no team to play for in the area where she lived. Could anything have been done to prevent this situation?

5. Share your thoughts about forms of corporate sponsorship involving companies that produce items like cigarettes, alcohol, and fast food. Do you think the following are acceptable, or not? Why?

a) In some countries, tobacco companies' logos are displayed at sports events where teenagers will be present.

b) Many sports teams for young children are sponsored by fast-food restaurants. These companies give money to children's sports, but they promote unhealthy eating.

c) Some stadiums are named after their sponsors, which are manufacturers of alcohol.

d) Beer is frequently advertised on television during the commercial breaks in major sports events.

Develop Speaking Fluency: Take Part in a Discussion 2
Agree and Disagree with Your Classmates

The education system in English-speaking countries is based on the idea that learning happens as a result of discussion. Students exchange ideas, and they agree and disagree about questions. This helps students to develop their ability to think critically and to arrive at an opinion that they have thought about carefully.

STRATEGIES FOR BEING A GOOD LISTENER

If you want to be a good speaker in class discussions, you first need to be a good listener. To be a good listener, you need to pay attention to your body language.

© ERPI • Reproduction prohibited

A. Work in pairs. Read the following tips for being a good listener. Fill in each blank with the correct word or phrase.

nod | lean back | eye contact | fold | interrupt | lean forward | personal space | stare

If you want to be a good listener, there are several things you should keep in mind.

1. Look at the person who is speaking. Make _____ with the speaker when possible, but don't _____. This will make the speaker feel nervous.

2. You should _____ your head to show that you are listening and that you understand what the speaker is saying, even if you don't agree.

3. It is helpful to _____ slightly to show that you are engaged in the conversation. Don't _____ in your chair because this suggests that you are not interested. However, be careful not to invade someone's _____.

4. Remember that you shouldn't _____ your arms. This puts distance between you and the speaker. Put your hands on the table.

5. Most importantly, don't _____ the speaker. Let the speaker finish. If you don't agree, you will have a chance later to express your own opinions.

If you follow these tips, you will be an excellent listener.

STRATEGIES FOR AGREEING AND DISAGREEING

B. Work in pairs. Read the following conversations.

Conversation A

John: I think corporate sponsorship has no place in children's sports. Children shouldn't be asked to advertise companies on their uniforms.

Sarah: I totally agree. They are too young to know what products they want to support. Companies should find other ways of advertising their stuff. They don't need to use kids' teams.

Grace: I know what you mean. I mean, what happens if a fast-food restaurant decides to sponsor a soccer team? I don't think it's a good idea for kids to be advertising burgers and fries. They need to learn to eat healthy food.

Kevin: Do you really think children pay attention to what's written on their soccer shirt? My little sister played on a kids' team when she was six years old, and her team was sponsored by a fast-food chain. It didn't mean she had to eat their food, did it?

Sarah: I see what you're saying, Kevin, but don't you think children are influenced by advertising? I know I was, when I was a kid. I wanted every product I saw in an ad.

Grace: I agree completely, Sarah.

© ERPI • Reproduction prohibited

Conversation B

Gus: This is great! All we have to do is lose to the Hawks in our last game, and we get the Tornados in the quarter final.

Bill: True. If we beat the Hawks, we get the Strikers in the quarter final, and they're a lot better than the Tornados. But we shouldn't try to lose a game. Don't you think we should try to win every game we play?

Angie: I think you're right, Bill. You guys have to try to win every time you play.

Gus: I see it differently. We can give our stars a rest and use some guys that don't usually play.

Ruby: I think that's a good point. You guys can beat the Tornados in the quarter final. You might not beat the Strikers.

Bill: I'm not sure I agree. For one thing, our confidence might go down if we deliberately lose a game. Plus, I think it would just make us look bad to everyone else if we lose on purpose.

Gus: OK, but don't you think getting to the finals is the most important thing?

Angie: You guys had better talk to the coach! You need to all agree on what you're doing.

Conversation C

Kira: I've just discovered this great supplement that is supposed to build up my muscles quickly! It should help me get ready for the tournament!

Mathilda: Isn't that illegal? Aren't you supposed to just compete without taking anything?

Kira: It's not illegal! It's brand-new! And it says there are no chemicals in it. I don't have to worry about drug testing if there are no drugs in it!

Mathilda: I guess that's true, but it sounds like it goes against the spirit of the competition. And even if they say this stuff doesn't have anything illegal in it, what if you find out later that it does? What then?

Kira: Yes, you have a point there. I don't want to end up in trouble. I guess I'd better just keep working out!

Mathilda: That's what I think, too. No one can beat you when you've been training hard!

C. With your partner, use the conversations above to find ways to agree, disagree, and admit someone is right.

Ways to agree with someone

1. _____

2. _____

3. _____

4. _____

5. _____

6. _____

Ways to disagree politely

1. _____

2. _____

3. _____

Ways to admit that someone else is right

1. _____

2. _____

MyBookshelf > My eLab > Exercises
> Unit 2 > Strategies

© **ERPI** • Reproduction prohibited

■ Improve Your Pronunciation: Which Word to Stress 2

A. Say this sentence: Freyja didn't want to play soccer in Vancouver.

In English, the **content words** (nouns, verbs, adjectives, and adverbs) are usually stressed.
Function words (pronouns, conjunctions, prepositions, articles, and auxiliary verbs) are not usually stressed.

You probably found that you stressed the nouns and verbs: *Freyja, want, play, soccer, Vancouver.*
This is normal. However, if you give one of these words more stress than usual, or if you stress a different word, you can change the meaning of the sentence.

B. Work in pairs. Listen to this sentence spoken with the stress in six different places. What is suggested by each sentence? What might the speaker say next?

1. _____

2. _____

3. _____

4. _____

5. _____

6. _____

MyBookshelf > My eLab > Exercises
> Unit 2 > Pronunciation

Bring It All Together

≥ **You are going to discuss several situations relating to sports. Follow the instructions below.**

1. Your teacher will set up discussion stations around your classroom. Each station has four participants and one situation for discussion. Refer to page 159 for the discussion situations.

2. Go to one of the stations. With your group, read the situation you are given, and discuss your opinion. Use the strategies you have learned. Use the space on the next page to make notes about your group discussions.

3. When your teacher tells you, move to another station. You will then work with a new group, and you will discuss a different situation.

4. Continue until you have visited each discussion station.

© ERPI • Reproduction prohibited

Sam's Baseball Team

Ben's Night Out

Johanna's Big Decision

Quinn's Choice

© **ERPI** • Reproduction prohibited

The Kings' Next Match

_____
_____
_____
_____
_____
_____
_____
_____

Robyn's Swimming Rival

_____
_____
_____
_____
_____
_____
_____
_____

USEFUL PHRASES

Agree with someone

I totally agree.

I know what you mean.

I agree completely.

I think you're right.

I think that's a good point.

That's what I think, too.

Disagree politely

I see what you're saying, but don't you think ...?

I see it differently.

I'm not sure I agree.

Admit that someone else is right

I guess that's true.

Yes, you have a point there.

HOW DID YOU DO?

Did you apply the strategies you have learned in this unit? Fill in the chart below to evaluate your own performance in this activity.

Strategy	Did I do this?		
	Yes	I'm not sure ...	No
I listened carefully to other students' opinions.			
I used suitable language to express my opinions.			

© **ERPI** • Reproduction prohibited

Strategy	Did I do this?		
	Yes	I'm not sure ...	No
I used suitable language to ask others what they thought.			
I used suitable language to agree and disagree.			
I was able to admit that someone else was right.			

Go Further

This is swimmer Michael Phelps. He has more Olympic medals than any other man, with a total of twenty-eight. However, his career was in danger in 2009 after a photo appeared in the media.

A. Work in groups of three or four. Use the Internet to answer the following questions.

1. What was Michael Phelps doing in the photo?

_____

2. Is this legal or illegal in sports?

_____

3. What punishment did Michael Phelps receive?

_____

4. In what other way did the event affect his career?

_____

5. What did he say about his behaviour?

_____

B. In your groups, discuss the following questions.

1. There have been several well-known cases of sports stars taking drugs. Why do you think this is the case?

2. Marijuana is not considered a performance-enhancing drug, but it is still banned in many sports. Why do you think it is banned? Should it be?

3. Do you think famous sportspeople have a responsibility to behave well? Explain your answer.

In this unit, you will learn to do the following:

Think critically about appearance and culture.

Use vocabulary related to clothing.

Keep a conversation going.

Distinguish between the /r/ and /l/ sounds.

APPEARANCE AND CULTURE

Discuss the Topic

A. Work in pairs. Discuss the following questions.

1. On what occasions do you (or people you know) wear traditional clothing?

_____

_____

_____

_____

_____

2. How do you feel when you (or other people) wear traditional clothing? Which of the following feelings are true for you? Write a check mark ✓ next to all that apply to you. Explain your answers to your partner.

☐ proud
☐ patriotic
☐ uncomfortable
☐ awkward
☐ other _____

3. How do attitudes toward traditional clothing differ between generations in your family?

_____

_____

_____

_____

4. Do you think people will continue to wear traditional clothing or decorate their bodies in traditional ways in the future? Why, or why not?

_____

_____

_____

_____

B. Have you ever seen someone from another culture wearing clothes from your culture, or styling their hair in a manner connected to your culture? If so, how did you feel? Discuss this question with your class.

© **ERPI** • Reproduction prohibited

Develop Your Vocabulary

A. Work in pairs. Look at the pictures of people in different clothes. Choose at least two adjectives for each picture. You may use words more than once.

colourful | stylish | classic | professional | traditional | modern
creative | unique | formal | handmade | casual | elegant

1. colourful, stylish, modern, creative, unique _____

2. _____

3. _____

4. _____

5. _____

6. _____

© **ERPI** • Reproduction prohibited

7. _____ 8. _____

B. Tell your partner what you would wear (or have worn) for the following situations:

1. An important interview for a job or university place.

2. Dinner with someone you are romantically attracted to.

3. A formal family event, such as your brother's or sister's wedding.

4. Dinner with your boyfriend's or girlfriend's parents.

5. A fourteen-hour plane journey in economy class.

6. The first day of classes in a new school year.

MyBookshelf > My eLab > Exercises
> Unit 3 > Vocabulary

Build Your Knowledge

BEFORE YOU READ

A. Discuss these questions with your class.

1. What is the woman in the photo wearing?

2. What do you know about this item of clothing?

© **ERPI** • Reproduction prohibited

B. Work in pairs. Read the paragraphs below. Put them in the correct order to tell the story of a young woman who found herself in trouble for wearing a dress from another culture.

Young Woman Criticized for Wearing Chinese Prom Dress

_____ Many people who expressed an opinion about Keziah's dress were American. But what did Chinese people think about the story? The *South China Morning Post*, a newspaper in Hong Kong, asked its readers: "Is it OK for non-Chinese people to wear *cheongsams*?" A huge majority—95 percent—of its readers said it was fine.

_____ There was an immediate response to Twitter pictures of her wearing the traditional Chinese dress. "My culture is NOT your *** prom dress," wrote Twitter user Jeremy Lam, in a tweet that was shared widely, and that was liked about 180,000 times. Many people agreed with him. Twitter users responded by saying that Keziah had no right to wear the dress when she didn't understand anything about its background or meaning in Chinese society. Some people said it wasn't right to wear the traditional clothing of any other culture other than one's own. This was, Twitter users argued, a form of cultural appropriation.

_____ Keziah repeatedly stated that she was not sorry for her choice of dress. As she told several media outlets, she had no regrets, and she would do it again. So, is wearing traditional clothing from another culture a form of cultural appropriation, or is it cultural appreciation? Whatever else the controversy caused by Keziah Daum's prom dress has meant, it has certainly raised some interesting questions.

_____ After the story was published in the media, Keziah became famous. She was interviewed on television, where she had a chance to explain her thinking. She also defended herself by posting on Twitter: "To everyone causing so much negativity: I mean no disrespect to the Chinese culture. I'm simply showing my appreciation to their culture … I've done nothing but show my love for the culture."

_____ When an American teenager named Keziah Daum decided to go shopping for a dress to wear for her high school dance, known as a "prom," she didn't want to go to a big department store and buy a typical formal dress. Instead, she went to a vintage clothing store and found an elegant red Chinese dress. The dress was a *qipao*, also called a *cheongsam*, and Keziah, eighteen, thought it was unique. When she got dressed up for her big night, she posted a number of pictures of herself wearing the dress on Twitter, as many modern teenagers do. And that's where the trouble began.

AFTER YOU READ

C. Work in pairs. Answer these questions.

1. What does the term "cultural appropriation" mean?

_____

2. Where did Jeremy Lam see the photo? How did he respond to Keziah?

_____

© **ERPI** • Reproduction prohibited

3. How many times was Jeremy Lam's comment liked on Twitter?

_____

4. How did Keziah respond to her critics?

_____

5. Keziah intended to act in a racist manner. True or false? Explain why.

_____

6. Would Keziah make the same choice again?

_____

D. Use your answers to the questions in task C to retell the story of Keziah and her dress in your own words.

MyBookshelf > My eLab > Exercises
> Unit 3 > Young Woman Criticized

Share Your Ideas

Join another pair to make a group of four. With your group, discuss the following questions.

1. As the reading says, the story about Keziah and her dress has attracted enormous interest around the world. Why do you think so many people are interested in this story?

2. Keziah's critics say she is guilty of cultural _appropriation_. Keziah says she is showing cultural _appreciation_. What do you think? On your own, decide where you would place Keziah's action on the line below. Then, compare your opinion with your group.

←———→

I think it was
okay to wear
the dress.

I think it was
wrong to wear
the dress.

3. Look at the following comments made on Twitter about Keziah's dress. How would you respond to each one?

> This isn't OK. I wouldn't wear traditional Korean, Japanese, or any other traditional dress, and I'm Asian. I wouldn't wear traditional Irish or Swedish or Greek dress either. There's a lot of history behind these clothes. Sad. **A**

> I'm a collector of _cheongsams_, with Chinese heritage, and I think it is ridiculous that other people are judging you! As Chinese, we are very proud and delighted to share our cultural fashions with anyone around the world. I love how you wear the dress with confidence! You rock! **B**

© ERPI • Reproduction prohibited

4. Do you ever wear clothes from another country or culture? If so, give some examples. Has your opinion about wearing these clothes changed since you read the story, or has it stayed the same?

5. Read the following response to the story and discuss the questions that follow.

Mike DeStefano
TUE 10:06 PM

I don't understand the anger toward Keziah. Our lives are full of things from other cultures. Every morning, I drink coffee from Colombia. I listen to reggae music from Jamaica while I drive to work in my Korean car. For lunch today, I might eat pizza from Italy or a taco from Mexico. I'm planning to go to an Italian restaurant for dinner tonight and watch a French film on my Japanese TV. We live in a time of globalization. Everything belongs to everybody these days.

a) Is there a difference between Keziah's dress and eating sushi or driving a Korean car? If so, why? If not, why not?

b) Do you agree that in a time of globalization, everything belongs to everybody? Explain your answer.

Develop Speaking Fluency: Take Part in a Discussion 3
Keep the Conversation Going

One of the most difficult aspects of discussion is keeping the conversation flowing. When you are discussing a topic with a group, you may decide that you all agree. What happens then? In a university or college class, you cannot simply say, "We all agree" and end the discussion. There may be almost an hour left in the class!

AWKWARD SITUATIONS

A. With your class, think of some times when you have found it difficult to keep a conversation going.

Example: It was the first day of a new semester at college. My classmates and I went for a cup of coffee in the break. I didn't know any of them, and I didn't know what to say to them.

1. _____

2. _____

3. _____

What strategies did you use to make sure the conversation continued?

© ERPI • Reproduction prohibited

A little silence is not a bad thing. Silence allows the members of the group to think about what has been said and to consider what to talk about next. However, too much silence is uncomfortable. There is always more that you can say about a topic. Here are some things you can do if things become quiet.

Ask open-ended questions.

If you run out of things to say, there is an easy solution: ask someone a question! The best kinds of questions to ask are open-ended questions that require more than a "yes" or "no" answer. When someone answers your question, don't just leave it there. Ask a follow-up question.

B. Work in pairs. Look at this conversation. Complete the conversation with expressions from the list.

Can you give me an example of what you mean? | What do you think should happen instead?
Why do you think that? | What exactly do you mean by that?

Adrienne: I'm going to the anti-fur protest in the town square. It's really important.

Michael: _____

Adrienne: We have to let people know that wearing fur is horrible. We want them to stop before they buy fur coats or other clothes.

Michael: _____
How are you going to stop them from buying those things?

Adrienne: We have signs, banners and a protest chant. It should make them think twice.

Michael: _____
How are signs or chants really going to stop people from buying clothes?

Adrienne: The idea is to show them it's socially unacceptable. Don't you think it's a good idea?

_____

Michael: I'd find some pictures of cute animals and wave them in their faces. That would make them really think about what they're doing because they'd see it for themselves.

© **ERPI** • Reproduction prohibited

Find a new way of looking at the topic.

There is always more than one way to look at a discussion topic. Try to consider the issue from someone else's point of view.

C. Now look at this conversation. Complete it with expressions from the list.

What would you do if you were in that situation? | Consider it from _____'s point of view.
Let's look at it another way. | Some people might not agree with that. They might say _____.

Greg: When I got my coffee this morning, the woman who served me had tattoos on both arms, and on her neck. She looked disgusting! I don't know why someone would want to do that to herself.

Tori: Well, that's just your point of view. _____
_____ A lot of people like tattoos because they see them as body art. It's not really any different than wearing their own kinds of clothes.

Greg: I don't like looking at tattoos. I'm sure a lot of customers don't. I don't know why they have servers who look like that.

Beatrix: _____
An employer can't refuse to hire someone just because of how they look.

Greg: When you're serving the public, how you look is important.

Tori: _____
we should accept people no matter what they look like.

Beatrix: _____
Would you tell someone you can't give them a job because of their tattoos?

Greg: It spoiled my coffee, that's all I can say.

Make connections.

Try to make a connection between the topic you are discussing and something else. For example, you could mention an experience you have had, or you could talk about something you read about online or in a newspaper.

D. Now complete this conversation with expressions from the list.

This reminds me of something I read. | I had a similar experience.
Something like that happened to my friend. | I saw something on the Internet about that.

Melody: You know what I really hate? The trend toward wearing pyjamas in public. I've seen people wearing their night clothes on the bus, in the cafeteria, even in lectures!

© **ERPI** • Reproduction prohibited

Brendan: I agree! _____
There's this website that shows pictures of real people wearing clothes that were far too casual for the situations they're in.

Adam: Cool. I walked into my Economics seminar the other day wearing a shirt and a tie because I wanted to look smart. Everyone thought I was on my way to a job interview.

Melody: _____
She wore a dress to class, and people asked her where she was going.

Brendan: _____
I wore a black jacket to a lecture, and someone asked me if I had been to a funeral. Can you believe it?

Adam: _____
I saw this article in a magazine where the author was talking about how we're all dressing far more casually these days than people did even a few years ago. The author's point was that …

MyBookshelf > my elab > Exercises
> Unit 3 > Strategies

Improve Your Pronunciation: Sounds /r/ and /l/

A. Say this sentence: Laura wore an elegant Italian dress to the prom.

For speakers of many languages, it can be difficult to distinguish between the /r/ and /l/ sounds. The main difference is that when you pronounce the /l/ sound, your tongue touches the top of your mouth. When you pronounce the /r/ sound, it does not.

B. Listen to the words. Underline the word you hear.

1. grass   glass   6. pirate   pilot
2. right   light   7. free   flee
3. rock   lock   8. grammar   glamour
4. race   lace   9. correct   collect
5. crown   clown   10. frame   flame

© **ERPI** • Reproduction prohibited

C. Work in pairs. Practise saying the following sentences.

1. Lily feels proud wearing her traditional Korean clothes.

2. Rory looks stylish in his classic raincoat.

3. Rosalind wears glasses in all the colours of the rainbow.

4. Leo wore his rubber boots to the playground because it was raining.

5. Lori loves jewellery, especially bracelets and earrings.

6. Renata's bright red leggings look silly.

7. You are not allowed to wear flip-flops in the restaurant.

8. Kerry makes creative clothes in orange and yellow.

D. Listen and repeat each sentence.

 MyBookshelf > My eLab > Exercises
> Unit 3 > Pronunciation

Bring It All Together

You are going to discuss several situations relating to clothes and culture. Follow the instructions below.

A. Read each situation. Think of one "yes" argument and one "no" argument for each. Make notes in the space below.

1. Ryan is a young man from Ireland. He is a big fan of reggae music, and he wears his hair in dreadlocks. This is a hairstyle associated with Rastafarians, a religious movement that started in Jamaica. Rastafarians see dreadlocks as a symbol of their African origin. Some of Ryan's friends have told him that he is wrong to choose this hairstyle, as it is not from his own culture. Should he cut off his dreadlocks?

Yes: _____

_____

No: _____

_____

© ERPI • Reproduction prohibited

2. Anika, twenty-two, is the daughter of immigrants in the United States. She enjoys modern dance and was recently invited to perform a solo dance in a show on campus. She invited her family to come and watch her. Instead of being proud of her, they were shocked to see her wearing shorts and a sleeveless shirt. Anika's family has told her she must not show her body in public in this way. She must respect her own culture. Are they right?

Yes: _____

_____

No: _____

_____

3. Jack is forty-three and has immigrated to the United Kingdom. He has changed his name to make it easier to pronounce, and he has found a job in computer sales. Jack wants to fit in with his new country, but he does not want to lose his own culture. He wears his own traditional clothes to work at his company. Jack's boss has told him that he cannot wear these clothes as they might make customers feel uncomfortable. Jack thinks this is racism. Is he right?

Yes: _____

_____

No: _____

_____

4. Emily is six years old and goes to school in Canada. Her Grade 1 teacher is planning a costume party for the children. There is one rule: the children must not wear costumes from another culture. For example, they are not permitted to dress up as Disney characters such as Princess Jasmine (Arabian) or Mulan (Chinese). Emily is unhappy because she wants to dress up as her favourite movie character, Pocahontas. Is the teacher right?

Yes: _____

_____

_____

No: _____

_____

© **ERPI** • Reproduction prohibited

5. Nick grew up in Australia. He bought a *keffiyeh* from another student at his university, and he likes to wear it around his neck. When he bought it, he did not know that this black-and-white scarf has a political meaning and is seen as a symbol of Palestine. Nick has never been to the Middle East, and he pays little attention to Middle Eastern politics. He just thinks his scarf looks cool with his black jeans and white shirt. Should he wear it?

Yes: _____

_____

_____

No: _____

_____

6. Betty, seventy-eight, lives in a seniors' community in Florida, USA. She bought a colourful sweatshirt in a used clothing store. It has a message on the front in a language Betty does not speak. Betty's grandson took a photo of Betty wearing her sweatshirt and showed it to some college friends. He was horrified to learn that Betty's sweatshirt had a rude message on the front. Betty says that none of her friends understand the words, and she likes the colour. Should she stop wearing this item?

Yes: _____

_____

No: _____

_____

B. Discuss these questions with a partner. Follow the instructions below.

1. Your teacher will arrange the seats in the classroom into two rows facing each other.

2. Your teacher will announce one question from the list above. Discuss the topic with the student sitting opposite you. You will have five minutes; try to keep the conversation going by asking open-ended questions, finding new ways to look at the topic, or making connections.

3. After five minutes, all students will move one seat to the right. You will now have a new partner. Your teacher will give you a new question for discussion.

C. After your pair discussions, discuss these topics with your whole class. Try to reach an agreement on what you think should happen.

© **ERPI** • Reproduction prohibited

USEFUL PHRASES

Ask open-ended questions

Can you give me an example of what you mean?

What do you think should happen instead?

Why do you think that?

What exactly do you mean by that?

Find a new way of looking at the topic

What would you do if you were in that situation?

Some people might not agree with that.
They might say _____.

Let's look at it another way.

Consider it from _____'s point of view.

Make connections

This reminds me of something I read.

I had a similar experience.

Something like that happened to my friend.

I saw something on the Internet about that.

HOW DID YOU DO?

Did you apply the strategies you have learned in this unit? Fill in the chart below to evaluate your own performance in this activity.

Strategy	Did I do this?		
	Yes	I'm not sure ...	No
I asked open-ended questions to keep the conversation going.			
I tried to look at situations from different perspectives.			
I made connections with other things I knew about.			

Go Further

This western woman has a tattoo on her neck in Chinese characters.

A. Work in groups of three or four. Use the Internet to answer the following questions.

1. Why do some non-Chinese people like to have tattoos in Chinese characters?

_____

_____

2. Which famous people have tattoos of Chinese characters?

_____

_____

3. Find some examples of Chinese character tattoos that don't mean what the wearer thinks they mean. Explain the examples.

_____

_____

_____

4. Are tattoos popular in China?

_____

_____

5. What are some possible health risks of getting a tattoo?

_____

_____

B. In your groups, discuss the following questions.

1. People who are not Chinese, who have no connection with Chinese culture, and who do not understand Chinese, shouldn't get Chinese tattoos. Do you agree or disagree? Why?

2. Apart from health concerns, what are some other negative effects of having a tattoo?

3. If you decided to have an English word or phrase tattooed on your body, what would it be?

© ERPI • Reproduction prohibited

In this unit, you will learn to do the following:

Think critically about current technology applications.

Use vocabulary related to technology.

Deal with challenging situations in group discussions.

Talk to group members in challenging situations.

Use intonation to identify whether or not a speaker is finished.

OLD TECH, NEW TECH

Discuss the Topic

A. On your own, look at the pictures in the chart. Do you know what each thing is? If you know the item, write its name above the picture. Do you use these items? Have you ever used them? Write a check mark ✓ in the correct column.

	I still use this.	I used this in the past, but not now.	I have never used this.	I don't know what this is.
1. _____				
2. _____				
3. _____				
4. _____				
5. _____				
6. _____				

→

© **ERPI** • Reproduction prohibited

	I still use this.	I used this in the past, but not now.	I have never used this.	I don't know what this is.
7. _____				
8. _____				

B. Work in groups of four. Share your answers with your group.

C. Can you think of anything else that was used in the past but not now? Discuss this question with your class.

Develop Your Vocabulary

A. Work in pairs. Use the clues to find new technological items. Use your dictionary where necessary. The first is done for you.

1. Oh no! I forgot my grandmother's birthday. I'll send her an e-_____card_____.
(birthday, anniversary, or graduation greetings that you send online)

2. No smoking is allowed on this flight. Please put away your e-_____.
(item that you smoke, that requires a battery)

3. If you have any e-_____, don't throw it in the garbage. Take it to a special recycling site. (old, unwanted electronic items, like computers)

4. Many traditional stores are closing down because of the rise in e-_____.
(business that is carried out online)

5. When you write an e-_____, especially at work, don't forget that spelling and grammar are still important. (letter sent online)

© ERPI • Reproduction prohibited

6. Have you ever ridden an e-_____? They are becoming popular these days. (two-wheeled motorized vehicle)

7. The library didn't have the book I need, but I can get it online as an e-_____. (text that you can read on your computer)

8. In this course, you will complete an e-_____ and submit it to your teacher at the end of the course. (collection of work that you keep on your computer and submit for a grade in a course)

9. Many colleges and universities are now offering opportunities for e-_____. (study carried out online)

10. If you take an e-_____ when you travel, you can load as many books on it as you like. You will save a lot of space in your luggage. (device that allows you to enjoy books in electronic format)

B. Tell your partner about the following:

1. How often you check your e-mail.

2. How your city or area deals with e-waste.

3. An example of e-learning that you have done, or that someone you know has done.

4. A time you or someone you know received an e-card.

5. What you think about using e-books instead of paper books.

6. If you know anyone who has tried an e-cigarette or something similar.

MyBookshelf > My eLab > Exercises
> Unit 4 > Vocabulary

Build Your Knowledge

BEFORE YOU WATCH

A. Discuss these questions with your class. Then, watch the video.

1. Have you been to a wedding recently? In what ways did technology play a role in the event?

2. How do people share memories of their weddings? What role does technology play?

3. What do you see as obvious uses for modern technology at weddings?

B. Watch the video. In this video, you will learn about how technology is changing weddings.

AFTER YOU WATCH

C. Work in pairs. Answer these questions.

1. What are some examples of unusual wedding locations shown in the video?

_____

_____

2. What are some types of new technology featured at the wedding of Taylor and Samantha Sinclair?

_____

_____

3. How did the bride and groom feel about all of the technology? Did they have any concerns?

_____

_____

4. What is a "doob"? What are doobs intended to replace?

_____

_____

5. What percentage of weddings now use drone photography? What does this tell you about the popularity of drones?

_____

_____

6. Explain the concept of the "modular wedding dress" as designed by Rebecca Schoneveld.

_____

_____

7. What does the "Wedding Happy" app do? What about the "Wedding Wire?"

_____

_____

© **ERPI** • Reproduction prohibited

MyBookshelf > My eLab > Exercises
> Unit 4 > Technology, This Year's Hottest
Wedding Trend

Share Your Ideas

> Join another pair to make a group of four. With your group, discuss the following questions.

1. Which of the technologies from the video do you think are the most useful in terms of weddings? Which do you think are pointless or silly? Write your answers below.

Useful	Pointless or silly

2. People often say things like this:

> Weddings are a time to be traditional: the dress, the cake, the photographs, the flowers, and of course, the happy couple. All this technology will destroy these traditions.

Do you think there is a danger of losing traditions by using so much new technology?

3. If you could talk with the couple in the video, what would you ask them about their use of technology at their wedding?

4. What are some of the other ways the technology shown in the video is being used now, or could be used in the future?
   a) drone photography
   b) 3-D modelling of people ("doob")
   c) list-making apps

5. a) (If you are married) What was your own wedding like? What role did technology play?

   b) (If you are not married) What do you imagine your future wedding will look like? What forms of technology are interesting to you?

© ERPI • Reproduction prohibited

Develop Speaking Fluency: Take Part in a Discussion 4
Deal with Things that Go Wrong

Any discussion runs the risk of something going wrong. This unit will show you how to use language to address problems that might arise in your discussions.

WHAT COULD GO WRONG?

A. Work in pairs. Look at the situations below and discuss how you would deal with each problem.

B. Take notes in the space beside each situation.

1. Vicky is in your group. She has plenty to say, but her pronunciation is very hard to understand. You aren't always sure what she is saying.

2. Carlos is very quiet. You know he has good ideas, but he rarely says more than "yes" or "no." You realize that he is very shy. You want to get him to share his opinions.

3. Elena has a lot to say and she often speaks faster and louder than the other students. Some of the other students find it hard to get into the conversation. When they do, Elena frequently interrupts them.

4. Jason doesn't seem interested in anything your group is talking about. He is constantly looking at his phone, falling asleep, or even leaving the room for a cigarette. You need the whole group to be involved in the discussion.

© ERPI • Reproduction prohibited

Someone is hard to understand.

Students like Vicky are often ignored. This is a pity because they may have valuable contributions to make to the discussion. Ignoring a speaker will make her feel terrible; it is likely that she is already embarrassed about her pronunciation.

It is not a good idea to say, "I don't understand you"; this will only make the speaker feel worse. It is also not helpful to ask the speaker to repeat, since you are unlikely to understand better the second time.

What can you do? A more successful strategy is to repeat the speaker's ideas in your own words, and then ask the speaker to confirm. Use language like this:

- So what you're saying, Vicky, is _____. Is that right?
- Are you saying that _____?

Is this you? Are you embarrassed about your own pronunciation? Don't be afraid to discuss this with your teacher and see if you can get some extra help.

Someone is too nervous to speak.

It can be hard to maintain a discussion with students like Carlos. As with Vicky, it is easy to ignore someone who doesn't play an active role in the conversation. However, this is a mistake as the person may have excellent contributions to make.

Encourage the person to speak up by being friendly: use his or her name, and smile. One way to encourage a good discussion is to use an open-ended question; ask a question that cannot be answered with "yes" or "no." Use language like this:

- Carlos, you said you agree. Why do you think this is the best solution?
- I think Carlos has a good point. Can you give us an example, Carlos?

Is this you? Don't worry about having perfect grammar—just focus on sharing your ideas. Your classmates will encourage you.

Someone dominates the discussion.

Some people, like Elena, are naturally more outgoing and love to talk. Some might talk a lot because they think they will get a better grade on the course. Sometimes, people who talk a lot will interrupt their classmates who are quieter and more reserved.

If you are not able to get into the conversation, pay attention to signals that a speaker is about to finish. If a talkative person picks up a coffee cup, leans back in their chair, or starts to hesitate (using "um …" or "uh …"), these are signs that you might be able to jump in. You may need to tell the speaker you haven't finished yet. Use language like this:

- Can I jump in here?
- Can I finish what I was saying?

Is this you? Remember that a good discussion relies on contributions from everyone. You will learn more if you develop an exchange of ideas with other students, rather than just telling everyone what you think. Focus on the quality of your statements, not on the amount of speech you produce.

© ERPI • Reproduction prohibited

Someone is not interested in the discussion.

If you are being given a group mark for a speaking assignment and one person, like Jason, is not doing any work, talk to him or her in private and find out what the situation is. It may be that the person is nervous about contributing; in this case, you can use the strategies discussed above.

On the other hand, if she or he is really not interested in the subject, the best thing to do is to talk through the subject in general. Perhaps there are aspects of the subject the person hasn't thought about, and would be interested in. Or maybe he or she hasn't heard anyone else say anything interesting. In any case, it's good to be encouraging. You can use language like this:

- Jason, is there some aspect to this you could talk about?

- Can we find an aspect of this that would interest you, Jason?

- I'd really like to hear what Jason has to say on this subject.

Is this you? If so, you will need to think carefully about why you are taking the course. What do you hope to get out of it? Is there some aspect to this assignment that you could contribute to? Remember, you are getting marked along with your group, so it's to your advantage to contribute to the discussion.

MyBookshelf > My eLab > Exercises
> Unit 4 > Strategies

■ Improve Your Pronunciation: Rising and Falling Tone

A. Say this sentence: If you want perfect wedding photographs, you should use a drone.

Notice how your voice rises at the end of the first part ("photographs") and then falls at the end of the second part ("drone"). Your intonation looks like this:

If you want perfect wedding photographs, you should use a drone.

If you hear a falling tone, you know that the speaker's statement is finished. This is your chance to jump in and respond.

If the speaker's voice does not fall, you know that the speaker has not finished. There is more to come. You should let the speaker finish.

B. Work in pairs. Listen to these statements. Decide whether each statement is finished (F) or unfinished (U).

1. The iPad was introduced by Apple founder _____

2. You can get married in the sky _____

3. A "doob" is a form of 3-D printing _____

4. New technology is exciting _____

5. Technology helps you at work and at home _____

6. Time travel might be possible one day _____

© ERPI • Reproduction prohibited

7. Guests at our wedding will be very surprised. _____

8. I would like a personal robot in my home. _____

C. Listen again and repeat each statement.

D. With your class, think of ways to end each unfinished statement. End each statement, paying attention to falling tone.

MyBookshelf > My eLab > Exercises
> Unit 4 > Pronunciation

Bring It All Together

A. Read about some new-technology products below. On your own, write the number of each product (1 to 10) in one of the columns in the table.

This product would improve my quality of life; I would like to own this.	This product looks like fun, but it's only for entertainment. I don't need it, but I would like to try it.	This might be useful for some people, but I would never buy this.	This product sounds like a waste of money—no one needs this!

1. Samsung's 146-inch television. Nicknamed "The Wall," this is the biggest television on the market. It is meant to hang on the wall and can even project multiple images.

2. Roidmi F8 vacuum cleaner. This is an ultra-light-weight upright vacuum cleaner which is extremely small and light. It comes with a smartphone app to measure performance.

3. Philips SmartSleep. This is a headset-type device that can be worn to promote a good night's sleep. The headset emits tones and vibrations that help the wearer fall asleep and sleep soundly.

4. Sony Xperia Touch. This small projector can turn any surface into an interactive touchscreen, so there is no need for an interactive whiteboard. It can be used anywhere.

5. Mix VR glasses. These virtual reality glasses are the most sophisticated ever produced for the gaming market. They are very light, and they connect to a laptop, tablet, or smartphone to improve the gaming experience.

© **ERPI** • Reproduction prohibited

6. Bandito. This is a device worn on the wrist that gets rid of mosquitoes. It is similar to a watch, but it puts out a smell that drives mosquitoes away. It can be worn for three months before needing a refill.

7. Combar camping tool. This versatile tool is like a giant-size version of a Swiss Army knife. The Combar combines an axe, shovel, knife, hammer, and saw in one tube-like piece of equipment.

8. Roam Ski. It fits over both legs and connects to an electronic sensor worn on the upper body. The Roam Ski helps skiers to adjust their position, making them better skiers and helping them get the best possible skiing experience.

9. Lumos bike helmet. This high-tech helmet comes with 48 LED lights, controlled by a remote on the handlebar. The bike rider can indicate left and right turns and also braking.

10. Hiuni telescope. This telescope for the digital age doesn't even have an eyepiece! Instead, the lenses search the night sky and display the pictures on the owner's connected tablet. It can also display information such as star charts on the tablet along with the pictures.

B. Work in groups of three or four. Compare your reactions to each of the products. What did you agree about? Where did you disagree?

C. What other technological innovation do you most wish were available? Use your imagination! With your group, complete the table.

Group member	Product you wish were available	What would need to happen to make it available?	Possibility (%) of the product existing in your lifetime

D. With your whole class, take a vote on the new item from C that you would most like to see.

© ERPI • Reproduction prohibited

USEFUL PHRASES

Make sure you understand someone.

So what you're saying, [name], is _____.
Is that right?

Are you saying that _____?

Encourage someone who is quiet.

[name], you said you agree. Why do you think
this is the best solution?

I think [name] has a good point. Can you give us
an example?

Make yourself heard.

Can I jump in here?

Can I finish what I was saying?

Bring someone into the conversation.

[name], is there some aspect to this you could
talk about?

Can we find an aspect of this that would interest
you, [name]?

I'd really like to hear what [name] has to say
on this subject.

HOW DID YOU DO?

Did you apply the strategies you have learned in this unit? Fill in the chart below to evaluate
your own performance in this activity.

	Did I do this?		
Strategy	Yes	I'm not sure ...	No
I made contributions to my group's discussion.			
I rephrased a classmate's remarks in my own words if I wasn't sure what they meant.			
I used open-ended questions to encourage others to participate.			
I asked someone to let me finish speaking if they kept jumping in during the discussion.			
I asked questions of students who didn't have much to say.			

© **ERPI** • Reproduction prohibited

Go Further

This is the Audi Pop.Up Next, part of the next generation of cars.

A. Work in groups of three or four. Use the Internet to answer the following questions.

   1. What is the Audi Pop.Up Next?

          _____

          _____

2. How fast can it travel? How is it powered?

_____

3. Who might benefit from having this product?

_____

4. Can you find some examples of cities or companies that are planning to use vehicles similar to this in the future?

_____

B. In your groups, discuss the following questions.

   1. Is the concept of "flying cars" realistic for everyone, or does it sound too much like science fiction?

   2. What are the possible good points about such a vehicle, and what are the bad ones? Make sure to thoroughly explore both points of view.

   3. How could cities and governments plan to make sure this technology will not be used in a harmful manner?

© **ERPI** • Reproduction prohibited

In this unit, you will learn to do the following:

Think critically about small homes.

Use vocabulary related to small homes.

Plan a presentation.

Design effective slides.

Give a short presentation on the topic of homes.

Distinguish between the voiced /ð/ and voiceless /θ/ *th* sounds.

LIVING SMALL

Discuss the Topic

A. Fill in the chart below with your own answers. Put a check mark ✓ in the correct place.

B. Then, survey your class. Walk around the room and ask your classmates questions like these:

- Do you live in a small home?
- Is your home in a safe neighbourhood?

C. Complete the chart with your classmates' answers.

	Yes	Not sure	No
1. I live in a small home.			
2. My home is in a safe neighbourhood.			
3. My home is close to stores and places for entertainment.			
4. My home is close to a park or other green space.			
5. I like the design and colours in my home.			
6. My home is quiet. I am not disturbed by noise.			
7. My home gives me a good feeling. I'm happy to be there.			
8. If I had more money, I would live in a larger home.			

D. What was the most surprising result of your survey? Discuss this question with your class.

© **ERPI** • Reproduction prohibited

Develop Your Vocabulary

A. Work in pairs. Look at the pictures. Choose two words from the list below to describe each picture. You may use words more than once. Then, add another word of your own to describe each picture.

trendy | urban | high-rise apartment | industrial building | historic | detached
mobile home | inexpensive | studio apartment | convenient | cramped | cabin
rural | loft | energy-efficient | houseboat

1. _____

_____

2. _____

_____

3. _____

_____

4. _____

_____

5. _____

_____

6. _____

_____

© ERPI • Reproduction prohibited

© ERPI • Reproduction prohibited

B. Tell your partner about the following:

1. Someone who might live in each of these homes.

2. The home on page 54 you would most like to live in.

3. The home on page 54 you would you least like to live in.

4. The best home you have ever had.

5. Where you hope to be living this time next year.

6. Where you hope to be living in five years' time.

MyBookshelf > My eLab > Exercises
> Unit 5 > Vocabulary

Build Your Knowledge

BEFORE YOU READ

A. Discuss these questions with your class.

1. What do you imagine a "tiny house" might look like?

2. What advantages to living in one room can you think of?

PAIR READING: TINY HOUSES AND MICROLOFTS

B. You are going to read about two kinds of small homes. Work in pairs. Student A: stay on this page. Student B: Turn to page 57.

You are Student A. Read about tiny houses, and answer your partner's questions.

Tiny Houses

The cost of new homes continues to rise. Many new housing developments are in the suburbs, far from urban centres. Many people are starting to ask why they should spend so much money for such a large house. The answer is the tiny house movement.

Tiny houses are defined as those under forty square metres. They are very simple, with only a cooking and eating space, a living space, and a sleeping space. The sleeping space is often under the roof and is reached by a ladder. These houses are the same size as a small apartment, but they are detached—there is no need to worry about noisy neighbours.

You cannot live in luxury in a tiny house. On the other hand, many people can afford them. You don't need to be a millionaire to own a tiny house. Many tiny house owners buy house plans and build some or all of the house themselves. These houses are also not expensive to maintain. The small size makes them energy-efficient, and the simple construction methods mean they are suited to all kinds of weather.

One special feature of tiny houses is that they can be moved. Many people who build tiny houses use trucks to move them to wherever they want to live. In some places, tiny house developments have appeared in urban centres. These houses are often owned by young people who don't want to live with their parents—they want their own homes. Tiny houses are also perfect for older people who want to "get away from it all" and live a quiet life in a rural area with no neighbours. All they need is a small amount of space!

Student A: Now, ask your partner these questions about microlofts. Write the answers.

1. What are microlofts? Where are they found?

_____

_____

2. How big are microlofts?

_____

_____

3. How do designers of microlofts make the best use of the space?

_____

_____

4. Who lives in microlofts?

_____

_____

5. What advantages do they have for this group?

_____

_____

6. What social problem might be helped by microlofts?

_____

_____

© **ERPI** • Reproduction prohibited

You are Student B. Read about microlofts, and answer your partner's questions.

Microlofts

For young people looking for housing they can afford in large urban centres, microlofts may be the answer. Microlofts are tiny one-room apartments. They are becoming popular in cities like New York, Vancouver, and San Francisco, where they are often located in abandoned industrial buildings or old hotels.

Microlofts may be only twenty square metres in size. But don't imagine a cramped space with no room to move. The designers of microlofts use a variety of techniques to make the most of the limited space. There are beds that pull down from the wall. There are coffee tables that convert into dining tables. The refrigerators, stoves, and dishwashers are smaller than average. Wall units hold electronic equipment like TVs. In some microloft buildings, four or five units share a kitchen. This leaves more space in the individual apartments.

It is possible to cook dinner for ten people in a microloft, but most tenants are not interested in large-scale entertaining. Microlofts are especially popular with millennials, those born between 1982 and 2004. They don't want a detached house in the suburbs. They want to be close to their workplaces, as well as to restaurants, movie theatres, and art galleries. Home is often just a place to sleep.

Living in a microloft is not only convenient, it is cheaper than an apartment. Many tenants are in their first jobs, or they are working hard to pay off student loans. There could even be another benefit of microlofts. These small homes could be an answer to the issue of homelessness, which is a problem in many urban centres.

Student B: Now, ask your partner these questions about tiny homes. Write the answers.

1. How big are tiny houses?

2. What can you find inside a tiny house?

3. Why is a tiny house better than an apartment?

4. How does living in a tiny house save people money?

© ERPI • Reproduction prohibited

5. What has appeared in some urban areas? Who lives there?

_____

_____

6. Why might tiny houses be popular with older people?

_____

_____

MyBookshelf > My eLab > Exercises
> Unit 5 > Tiny Houses and Microlofts

Share Your Ideas

Join another pair to make a group of four. With your group, discuss the following questions.

1. Would you like to live in a tiny house or microloft? Why, or why not?

2. What are the advantages of living in a smaller space? Use information from both readings to complete the table with six more advantages. The first is done for you. After, rank these advantages from most important (1) to least important (5).

Advantages	Ranking
Small homes use less energy.	

© **ERPI** • Reproduction prohibited

3. Look at the following arguments against living in small homes. How would you respond to each one?

> Small homes are not real homes. People need to be surrounded by lots of personal belongings to feel comfortable. **A**

> Small homes don't encourage communities to grow. People who live in small homes often move around. This is bad for society. **B**

> Small homes might be cheaper, but it's hard to entertain guests in a small home. You'll just end up going out more often to restaurants. **C**

4. In many parts of the world, society is changing. There are more single-parent families, childless couples, and active retired people. How might this change the kinds of homes that people want to live in?

5. What do you think will be the main trends in housing in the next fifty years? Why?

Develop Speaking Fluency: Give a Presentation 1
Plan an Effective Presentation

In this unit, we will turn our attention to giving a presentation to the class. The first aspect of presentations we will look at is planning your presentation.

PLANNING THE PRESENTATION

A. Watch the video entitled *Life on a Houseboat*. Then, with a partner, complete the outline below to show how the speaker organizes the presentation.

Introduction: _____

First point: _____

    Information: _____

    _____

    _____

Second point: _____

    Information: _____

    _____

    _____

© ERPI • Reproduction prohibited

Third point: _____

Information: _____

_____

_____

Fourth point: _____

Information: _____

_____

_____

Fifth point: _____

Information: _____

_____

_____

Conclusion: _____

_____

_____

STRATEGIES FOR PLANNING YOUR PRESENTATION

B. Watch the video again. Look at the following strategies. With your partner, discuss what the speaker does.

Strategy	What does the speaker do?
1. Start with an introduction.	• Greets the audience. • _____ • _____
2. Explain any background information your audience may need.	• _____ • _____
3. Use phrases that signal that you are moving on to a new idea.	• Uses expressions such as: _____ _____ _____ _____

© ERPI • Reproduction prohibited

Strategy	What does the speaker do?
4. Involve your audience.	• _____ _____ _____
5. End with a conclusion.	• _____ • _____ • _____

C. Discuss your answers with your class.

DESIGNING YOUR SLIDES

As you plan your presentation, you should think carefully about what you are going to put on your slides. What information, colour, and pictures are you going to use?

D. Work in pairs. Look at the slides below. For each one, discuss (a) what you like about it, and (b) what improvements you might suggest.

Slide A

ADVANTAGES OF LIVING ON A HOUSEBOAT

There are many advantages to living on a houseboat. Although boats are expensive, they cost less than houses, so people often own their own boats outright, with no loans from the bank. There's not much housekeeping, since boats have small interiors and are easy to clean. Living on a boat provides a unique lifestyle for people who like being on the water. A lot of regular costs, e.g., electricity and water, are less for a boat. Living on a boat saves money on vacations because people can take their boat for a trip. In conclusion, there are many reasons why living on a houseboat is a good choice.

What we like about this slide	How it could be improved

© **ERPI** • Reproduction prohibited

Slide B

One of the great things about life on a boat is how compact it is. There's no wasted space and no need for a lot of interior decorating or upkeep.

Boat living is fun and popular in many places around the world. It's cheaper than living in a house, so many boat users own their boats outright.

Many boat users live at marinas where they can hook their boats up to electricity and water. So they don't miss any of the comforts of home while still living on the water! Marinas are also great places to socialize and meet people.

The best part of life on a boat for most people is simple: they can head out on a trip any time they want.

What we like about this slide	How it could be improved

Slide C

ADVANTAGES OF LIVING ON A BOAT

- Cheaper than a house—no bank loans.
- Easy to maintain and keep clean.
- Electricity and water cost less for a boat.
- No need to go on vacation.
- A great view.
- A unique lifestyle.

© **ERPI** • Reproduction prohibited

What we like about this slide	How it could be improved

E. Now, with your partner, use your ideas to develop some guidelines for designing effective slides. Fill in the chart with things you should and should not do.

When you are designing slides, you should ...	When you are designing slides, you should not ...

MyBookshelf > My eLab > Exercises
> Unit 5 > Strategies

© **ERPI** • Reproduction prohibited

Improve Your Pronunciation: *Th* Sounds /ð/ and /θ/

A. Say this sentence: A tiny house? I think that's a great idea!

One of the most challenging sounds in English is *th*. This sound can appear at the beginning of a word, in the middle of a word, or at the end of a word.

To make the *th* sound, your lips should be slightly open, and your tongue should touch the top of your mouth just behind your front teeth. You can also put your tongue between your teeth; this will give you the same sound.

There are actually two *th* sounds in English:

a) The "voiced" *th*, written as /ð/; this is the sound you hear in words like *this*, *that*, *then*, *with*, *together*, and *those*.

b) The "voiceless" *th*, written as /θ/; this is the sound you hear in words like *think*, *theatre*, *thousand*, *thank*, *both*, *birthday*, and *something*.

The difference is that the vocal chords vibrate when you pronounce a voiced sound.

B. Work in pairs. Complete the table with other words that you know. If you are not sure which sound you are making, ask yourself whether or not you can hear a vibration. Which pair can find the most words?

	Beginning of word	Middle of word	End of word
Voiced *th* /ð/			
Voiceless *th* /θ/			

C. Listen to the words. Do you hear a voiced or a voiceless *th*? Underline your answer.

1. Voiced /ð/   Voiceless /θ/   **7.** Voiced /ð/   Voiceless /θ/

2. Voiced /ð/   Voiceless /θ/   **8.** Voiced /ð/   Voiceless /θ/

3. Voiced /ð/   Voiceless /θ/   **9.** Voiced /ð/   Voiceless /θ/

4. Voiced /ð/   Voiceless /θ/   **10.** Voiced /ð/   Voiceless /θ/

5. Voiced /ð/   Voiceless /θ/   **11.** Voiced /ð/   Voiceless /θ/

6. Voiced /ð/   Voiceless /θ/   **12.** Voiced /ð/   Voiceless /θ/

© ERPI • Reproduction prohibited

D. Work in pairs. Practise saying the following sentences.

1. It's better to be healthy than wealthy.

2. Their father is the weatherman on the television.

3. This is my tenth toothache this week.

4. Thank you for my birthday card. It was very thoughtful.

5. Elizabeth went to the theatre on Thursday.

6. Dorothy is running the North Bay marathon next month.

7. The youth club members hiked along the path with their guide.

E. Listen and repeat each sentence.

MyBookshelf > My eLab > Exercises
> Unit 5 > Pronunciation

Bring It All Together

A. Design a short presentation on the following topic:

- Think about the homes of the future. How will people live in fifty years' time? What will their homes look like? What will be inside their homes? Where will they be located?

You should aim for six to eight slides.

B. Work in groups of three. Present your talk to your classmates and listen as they present theirs.

HOW DID YOU DO?

Did you apply the strategies you have learned in this unit? Fill in the chart below to evaluate your own performance in this activity.

Strategy	Did I do this?		
	Yes	I'm not sure ...	No
I started with a clear introduction.			
I explained any necessary background information.			
I used pictures and colour carefully.			
I used bullet points, not complete sentences.			
My slides could be read by people at the back of the room.			
I ended with a conclusion where I summarized my ideas.			

© ERPI • Reproduction prohibited

Go Further

This is Miranda Gibson, an Australian teacher. From 2011 to 2013, Miranda spent 449 days living in a tree.

A. Work in groups of three or four. Use the Internet to answer the following questions.

1. Why did Miranda live in a tree?

_____

_____

_____

2. What was her tree home like? What did she have? What did she not have?

_____

_____

_____

3. What did she eat while she was living in the tree?

_____

_____

4. Why did she come down from the tree?

_____

_____

5. What environmental success was achieved after she left the tree?

_____

_____

B. In your groups, discuss the following questions.

1. Do you think Miranda did the right thing by living in the tree? What else could she have done?

2. Do actions like this have positive results, or are they just a way to get attention?

3. Does this situation remind you of any other case you might have heard about where someone spent time living in a difficult situation because of his or her beliefs? What happened?

© **ERPI** • Reproduction prohibited

In this unit, you will learn to do the following:

Think critically about starting and running a business.

Use vocabulary related to entrepreneurship.

Develop skills in delivering a presentation.

Give a short presentation to your class.

Pronounce the ends of words.

BECOMING AN ENTREPRENEUR

Discuss the Topic

A. Work in pairs. Read the following stories of entrepreneurs. Use the clues in each paragraph to guess the entrepreneur's company from the list below. One is extra.

KFC | Rawfully Organic | Cambridge Satchel Company | SlideShare
Amazon | Leanna's Essentials | IKEA | Colorblind Cards | Apple

1. Ingvar Kamprad founded his furniture company at the age of seventeen and sold replicas of his uncle's table by mail order. He opened his first store in 1965 and built his company into a multinational empire. Although he was worth $15 billion in his later years, he lived in a modest home and took the bus. Kamprad died in 2018 at the age of ninety-one. In his will, he left a large amount of money for development projects in Sweden.

   Company: _____

2. At the age of sixteen, Kristina Carrillo-Bucaram was diagnosed with a medical condition; she became a vegan and committed to a diet of raw foods. In university, she established a farmer's market. This led to a company that sells fruit juices. However, Kristina is best known for her social media presence, particularly her YouTube channel, FullyRawKristina. She has also published a bestselling book on raw foods.

   Company: _____

3. Jeff Bezos decided to found an online bookstore in 1993 with $300,000 from his parents. His company grew and expanded into other areas, such as music and videos, and by 1999 he was a billionaire. He almost went bankrupt in 2002, but the following year he was again making a profit. In 2016, the company started by Bezos was named the largest online shopping retailer, and in 2018, Bezos was named the richest person in the world.

   Company: _____

4. Jessica Huie has an English mother and a Jamaican father. As a member of a minority group, Jessica was shocked that she couldn't find a birthday card in multicultural London with a picture of a child who looked like her dark-skinned daughter. This prompted her to start a company that produces cards showing people of various races and ethnic backgrounds.

   Company: _____

5. As a young man, Harland Sanders had many jobs, but it was while running a gas station that he decided to cook some of his favourite foods for customers. Eventually he came up with his own recipe for chicken. This became so popular that he opened a chain of restaurants, using the franchise system, where other people pay a fee to open a branch of the restaurant. After starting to sell franchises at sixty-five, he finally sold the chain at seventy-three.

   Company: _____

© ERPI • Reproduction prohibited

6. Julie Deane's daughter was being bullied in school, and Julie wanted to send her to a private school. Julie wanted to start a business—but what kind of business? Her children asked for traditional school bags, like those carried by Harry Potter and Hermione Granger, and Julie couldn't find them anywhere. She had her business idea! Within five years, Julie's business was worth $65 million—more than enough to pay private school tuition fees.

Company: _____

7. Rashmi Sinha initially studied psychology, but she later became interested in computer science. With her husband and her brother, in 2006 she established an online site where people can upload the slides from presentations they have given at meetings and conferences. The site became very popular in a short period of time. Rashmi sold it in 2012 for over $100 million.

Company: _____

8. Leanna Archer owes her success to her great-grandmother from the Caribbean island of Haiti. At the age of nine, Leanna started to make hair-care products using natural ingredients and her great-grandmother's secret recipe. She gave a few samples to her friends, and the word about her products spread. By the time she was sixteen, she was making $100,000 a year. She uses some of her profits to support her own charity, which helps children in Haiti.

Company: _____

B. Which of the entrepreneurs are you most impressed by? Why? Discuss this question with your class.

Develop Your Vocabulary

A. Work in pairs. Choose the best word to complete each of the following sentences.

entrepreneur | founded | shares | competitor | bankrupt
profit | expand | market | franchise | invest

1. Farah's Fine Foods opened new stores in Asia because it knew there was a _____

there for its products.

2. After all the investors withdrew their money, the IXB Corporation went _____

and had to go out of business.

3. Ruth was an _____ when she was a teenager, as she sold handmade

jewellery to students at her school.

© ERPI • Reproduction prohibited

4. After years of being the only shoe store in town, The Shoe Spot now has a _____ called The Shoe Tree.

5. Beckford Manufacturing had a very successful year last year, making its biggest _____ in its twenty-year history.

6. Joey's Burgers was _____ with one restaurant in 1945; fifty years later, there were thousands of restaurants all over the world.

7. The cost to buy a new doughnut shop _____ has risen to almost $1 million, which is hard to imagine.

8. A wealthy businesswoman bought a majority of the _____ in Healthyjuice, and now she controls it.

9. Mamma's Italian restaurant needs someone to _____ a lot of money into it if it is going to succeed.

10. The Fashion Market plans to _____ so that it can start to sell children's clothing.

B. Tell your partner about the following:

1. An entrepreneur from your country that you admire.

2. The kind of business you would invest money in if you could.

3. A place you used to shop in that went bankrupt.

4. An international company that has expanded recently in your home country.

5. A franchise business you regularly go to, such as a store or fast-food restaurant.

6. A business that was founded by a friend or relative.

MyBookshelf > My eLab > Exercises
> Unit 6 > Vocabulary

© **ERPI** • Reproduction prohibited

Build Your Knowledge

A. Discuss these questions with your class. Then, watch the video.

1. What image comes to your mind when you hear the title "Chief Executive Officer," or "CEO"?

2. If you heard that a sixteen-year-old boy or girl was a CEO, how would you react?

3. What kind of company could be run by someone who is sixteen years old?

VIDEO: SIXTEEN-YEAR-OLD DROPOUT IS CEO OF COMPANY POTENTIALLY WORTH MILLIONS

B. Watch the video. In this video, you will learn about a sixteen-year-old boy, Ben Pasternak, who is the CEO of his own company.

AFTER YOU WATCH

C. Work in pairs. Answer these questions.

1. What is the name of Ben's company? What kind of company is it?

   _____

   _____

2. What two dramatic decisions did Ben make in order to develop his business?

   _____

3. Which celebrity follows Ben on Twitter? Does Ben follow this person back?

   _____

4. What do you learn about Ben's relationship with his parents?

   _____

   _____

5. What do the following people say about Ben?

   a) His main employee

   _____

   _____

   b) His main investor

   _____

© ERPI • Reproduction prohibited

6. Which companies does Andrew Nusca compare Flogg to?

_____

7. Does Ben want to be like Mark Zuckerberg? Why, or why not?

_____

Share Your Ideas

Join another pair to make a group of four. With your group, discuss the following questions.

1. In what ways is Ben typical of a sixteen-year-old? In what ways is he different?

2. Do you think Ben will regret dropping out of school at some point? Why or why not?

3. Ben's grandfather is a wealthy property developer worth over $300 million. Look at the comment below. Do you agree or disagree with it? Why?

> It's not surprising that Ben's company is a success. He comes from a wealthy background. He was born with good business sense. Running a business is in his DNA!

4. If you could ask Ben any question about his success or his future plans, what would you ask him?

5. Look at the following factors which might contribute to the long-term success or failure of an entrepreneur. On your own, rank them in order from most important (1) to least important (5). As you decide, think about people you know who have been successful in business. Then, discuss your ranking with your group.

_____ having an original idea

_____ being lucky

_____ working hard

_____ understanding business

_____ knowing a lot of people

Can you think of any other factors that contribute to entrepreneurial success?

6. Since this video was made in 2016, Ben Pasternak has stopped focusing on the company in the video and has moved on to new projects. In 2016, he launched a video chat app called Monkey, which he sold to a Chinese competitor in 2017. Based on what you know about Ben, what do you predict he will be doing five years from now?

MyBookshelf > My eLab > Exercises
> Unit 6 > Sixteen-Year-Old Dropout

© **ERPI** • Reproduction prohibited

Develop Speaking Fluency: Give a Presentation 2
Speaking in Front of the Class

This unit focuses on giving the presentation. Here, we will look at your speaking style and your body language.

STRATEGIES FOR DEALING WITH NERVES

There is no doubt that speaking in public can be nerve-wracking. Fear of speaking in public is called "glossophobia" and is estimated to affect 75 percent of people. Have you ever seen a speaker who was playing with their hair, crumpling their paper, clicking their pen, or pacing back and forth? These are all signs of nerves. Being nervous is common, but there are things you can do to help yourself.

A. Work in pairs. Look at the following advice for dealing with nerves before giving a presentation. With your partner, decide which advice you think is useful, and which is not useful.

Advice	Useful	Not useful
1. Memorize every word of your presentation.		
2. Think of a good joke to make your audience laugh.		
3. Practise your presentation with friends.		
4. Eat something before the presentation.		
5. Arrive early at the presentation room.		
6. Make sure your technology works before you start.		

STRATEGIES FOR SPEAKING TO A GROUP

B. Watch the video, "The Man Who Gives Away Shoes, Version 1." With a partner, decide what you like or dislike about the way in which the speaker gives the presentation. Choose your best answer to each statement.

Speaker	Version 1			Version 2		
	Yes	Not sure	No	Yes	Not sure	No
1. The speaker looked relaxed and comfortable.						
2. The speaker made eye contact with the audience.						

© **ERPI** • Reproduction prohibited

Speaker	Version 1			Version 2		
	Yes	Not sure	No	Yes	Not sure	No
3. We could hear the speaker clearly.						
4. The speaker spoke at the right speed.						
5. The speaker paused at appropriate times.						
6. The speaker moved around the room.						
7. The speaker used hand gestures appropriately.						
8. The speaker smiled.						

C. Now watch "The Man Who Gives Away Shoes, Version 2." With your partner, choose the best answer for each statement for Version 2.

D. Based on the videos you have just watched, decide whether you should do each of the items in the table below. On your own, choose the best answer for each statement. Then compare your answers with your partner.

Giving a Presentation	Yes	No	Maybe
1. Write out every word of your presentation, so you can read it.			
2. Dress up for the presentation.			
3. Start with an apology for not being a native speaker of English.			
4. Look at your audience during the presentation.			
5. Speak slowly.			
6. Pause often to give your audience a chance to think about what you are saying.			
7. Smile a lot.			
8. Move around the room.			
9. Use your hands to help you make points as you talk.			

© ERPI • Reproduction prohibited

STRATEGIES FOR ANSWERING QUESTIONS FROM THE AUDIENCE

First, decide (or ask your teacher) whether questions will be allowed during the presentation or whether anyone with a question should wait to the end. Make sure everyone knows what is expected.

E. Work in pairs. Look at the situations below and decide what advice you would give to each speaker.

1. Caitlin is not nervous about giving her presentation, but she is worried about the question-and-answer session afterwards. If you are in this situation, and someone asks you a question that you cannot answer, what can you do?

_____

_____

2. The last time Joel gave a presentation, someone asked a question that led to a discussion unrelated to Joel's topic. He felt that he had lost control of his own talk. What can you do if this happens to you?

_____

_____

STRATEGIES FOR ANSWERING QUESTIONS

You don't know the answer.

You could try to predict some of the questions you might be asked and plan your answers in advance. If you get a question that you cannot answer, you should be honest and tell the person asking the question that you are not sure. Don't make up an answer!

Say that you will check, and you will get back to the questioner later with more information. You can also see if anyone else in the audience wants to contribute. Use language like this:

- I'm not sure, but I'll get back to you later.

- I don't immediately have an answer to that. Does anyone else know?

Someone takes your presentation in a different direction.

You need to be strong and stand up to the person who is taking over your talk. It is your responsibility to stay in control of your presentation. You will need to tell the questioner that you have to focus on the topic of your presentation. Use language like this:

- Can I come back to what I was talking about?

- That's interesting. We can talk about that later. Let's focus on …

MyBookshelf > My eLab > Exercises
> Unit 6 > Strategies

© ERPI • Reproduction prohibited

■ Improve Your Pronunciation: Pronounce the Ends of Words

A. Say this sentence: His company provides shoes for children in need.

Did you pronounce the end of every word? In English, many words end with a consonant (*his, shoes, need*), or with a group of consonants, known as a consonant cluster (*provides*). It is very important to pronounce these end-of-word consonants.

If you are finding it difficult to understand a classmate's presentation, it may be because the speaker is dropping these final consonants and saying, for example, *shoe, provi−*, or *nee−*. This can happen when someone is nervous and is speaking quickly. It can also happen when someone's first language doesn't emphasize consonants at the ends of words.

B. Work in pairs. Practice saying these pairs of words.

1. see	seat		**6.** tree	treat
2. buy	bite		**7.** may	make
3. dry	drive		**8.** how	house
4. free	freeze		**9.** low	load
5. go	goat		**10.** say	save

C. Listen to the following sentences, and repeat each one, paying attention to the sounds at the end of each word. With your partner, practise saying them.

1. Bill Gates dropped out of university and established Microsoft. He was later named the richest person in the world.

2. Leanna gave samples of her hair-care products to her friends. She was shocked when they asked for more. She decided to invest money in starting a business.

3. Clint's restaurant made a modest profit for the first two years, but then he went bankrupt. His chefs and servers all lost their jobs.

4. I've received so many texts advertising sales at the mall. This is the sixth one today! What a waste of time.

5. Colorblind Cards was one of the first companies to make greeting cards for customers of different races.

MyBookshelf > My eLab > Exercises
> Unit 6 > Pronunciation

Bring It All Together

A. Design a short presentation on one of the following topics:

a) How to be a successful entrepreneur

b) Another topic you have looked at so far in this course

c) A topic of your own choice (check with your teacher)

You should aim for twelve to fifteen slides. As you design your slides, keep in mind the tips on pages 59 to 63 about designing an effective slide presentation.

B. Present your talk to your class. Your presentation should take around ten minutes. You should be prepared to answer questions from the audience after your presentation.

HOW DID YOU DO?

Did you apply the strategies you have learned in this unit? Fill in the chart below to evaluate your own performance in this activity.

Strategy	Did I do this?		
	Yes	**I'm not sure ...**	**No**
I wrote my presentation in point form.			
I practised my presentation before I gave it.			
I ate something before the presentation.			
I arrived at the presentation room in good time.			
I checked my technology before I started.			
I dressed appropriately.			
I looked at people in all sections of the room.			
I spoke slowly enough that people could follow me.			
I paused to allow people to think about my talk.			
I moved around appropriately—not too much or too little.			
I used my hands appropriately.			
I answered questions from the audience well.			

© **ERPI** • Reproduction prohibited

Go Further

This is entrepreneur Salman (Sal) Khan, who founded an online business. But Khan is not motivated only by making money.

A. Work in groups of three or four. Use the Internet to answer the following questions.

1. What does Salman Khan's company do?

_____

_____

_____

2. What is Salman Khan's background? How did he come to establish his company?

_____

_____

_____

3. Is Khan's business successful? How do you know?

_____

_____

4. How much do Khan's products cost? Why?

_____

_____

5. Give an example of students who have been helped by Khan's products.

_____

_____

B. In your groups, discuss the following questions.

1. What do you think motivates Khan to help so many people?

2. Do you think entrepreneurs have a responsibility to use their money to help others? Why, or why not?

3. Can you think of any other successful entrepreneurs who give away products or money?

© **ERPI** • Reproduction prohibited

ANSWERS

Strategies: task A page 73

1. Not useful. It is fine to have notes on a piece paper to refer to, but trying to memorize every word will make you more nervous.

2. Not useful. There is nothing worse than a situation where someone tells a joke and no one laughs. Don't try it.

3. Useful. If you practice your presentation, you will check that your timing is right, and you will be sure about the pronunciation of words you are using. Your friends might even give you some valuable feedback.

4. Useful. However, do not overeat, or you will be uncomfortable. Needless to say, don't drink alcohol before your talk, even if you think it will relax you.

5. Useful. Arrive in good time, don't arrive too early. If you are too early, waiting outside the room will make you more nervous. Make sure you are there to greet your classmates as they arrive.

6. Useful. Always make sure your technology is working and that you know how to use it. Many presentations have been ruined by technical problems.

Strategies: task D page 74

1. No. A presentation is not the same as an essay. If you write every word, you will end up reading your presentation, not speaking to your audience.

2. Maybe. You don't need to wear a suit or a dress, but you should look smart and tidy.

3. No. Even if you are nervous about your English, never apologize to your audience.

4. Yes. A common piece of advice is to follow a W shape: look at people in the back left corner, then the front left corner, the back centre, and so on. Don't focus on one person. In particular, don't look at your teacher and ignore your classmates.

5. Yes. You know your topic, but your classmates do not. They need time to process your information. If you feel that you are speaking too slowly, your speed is probably right.

6. Yes. Again, your classmates need time to absorb your information. A few brief pauses can be helpful. It can be a good idea to pause to have a sip of water.

7. Maybe. Certainly, it is nice to smile, but if you smile constantly, you might appear nervous. You want to show that you are confident.

8. Maybe. You don't need to stand in one spot, but don't walk around too much either. A few steps are fine. Don't walk too far from your microphone (if you have one).

9. Maybe. One of the hardest things about speaking in public is knowing what to do with your hands. The best thing is to hold your notes in your hands, and to use them when you want to make a particular point. For example, if you want to draw the audience's attention to a picture on a slide, use your hands to gesture to the picture. If you are using an interactive whiteboard, don't touch the screen until you are ready to move to the next slide.

© **ERPI** • Reproduction prohibited

In this unit, you will learn to do the following:

Think critically about differences between customs in different cultures.

Use vocabulary related to travel and customs.

Learn about the dynamics of groups.

Learn strategies to develop collaboration skills.

Take part in a group problem-solving activity.

Link words together.

TRAVEL AND CUSTOMS

Discuss the Topic

A. In some countries there are things you should or should not do. Your teacher will give you the answer to ONE of these questions. Find a classmate who has the answer to the others. Fill in the answers below.

Example: Student A: In what country should I take off my shoes in someone's house?

Student B: I don't know, sorry.

Student A: In what country should I take off my shoes in someone's house?

Student C: I know that one. It's _____.

Student A: How do you spell that?

---

1. Always take your shoes off when you go into someone's house in _____.

2. If you see a cute child in _____, you must not touch him on the head.

3. Don't give someone a thumbs-up sign in _____. It is a very rude gesture.

4. In _____, do not use your left hand to give something to someone.

5. In _____, don't hold hands with your boyfriend or girlfriend in public.

6. Remember that it is illegal to chew gum in _____.

7. If you visit someone's home in _____, don't bring an even number of flowers (6, 8, 10, etc.).

8. Don't blow your nose in public in _____.

9. If you visit a church in _____, always cover your knees and shoulders.

10. Chefs in _____ will be upset if you put salt on your food.

11. In _____, don't talk about your work at dinner time.

12. If you go to a restaurant in the _____, always tip at least 15 to 20 percent.

13. In _____, don't wish someone a happy birthday before the actual day.

14. Don't raise your arm to wave to someone in _____.

15. In the _____, don't raise two fingers to indicate the number "2".

16. In _____, never pour yourself a drink without offering a drink to the others at your table.

17. In _____, if you nod your head, you mean "no." If you shake your head, you mean "yes."

18. Never sit on a table in _____.

19. In _____, it is considered rude to chew gum while talking.

20. In _____, you must treat a book with respect. Don't write in it, and don't put it on the ground.

© ERPI • Reproduction prohibited

B. Where are all of these countries? Can you find them on a map? Discuss your answers to task A with your class.

Develop Your Vocabulary

A. Work in pairs. Match each word with the correct meaning.

Words		Meanings
1. exotic (adjective)		**a)** the action of welcoming guests
2. sacred (adjective)		**b)** typical way of behaving in a certain society
3. hospitality (noun)		**c)** country that is governed by a more powerful country
4. ancient (adjective)		**d)** with special religious meaning
5. respect (verb)		**e)** make an effort not to do something
6. colony (noun)		**f)** not changing for a long time
7. custom (noun)		**g)** very old
8. avoid (verb)		**h)** place that travellers enjoy visiting
9. traditional (adjective)		**i)** unusual because it is from another country
10. tourist attraction (noun)		**j)** follow established rules

B. Now, with your partner, use each word from A to make a sentence about each of the countries below. Use each word and each country once.

Example: In India, the cow is a sacred animal.

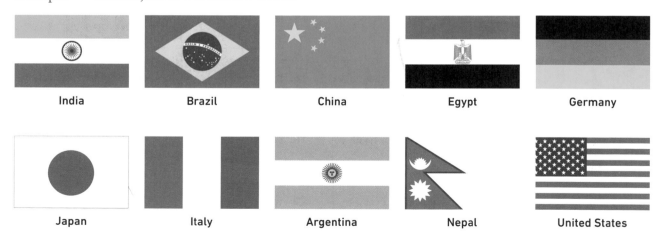

India   Brazil   China   Egypt   Germany

Japan   Italy   Argentina   Nepal   United States

© ERPI • Reproduction prohibited

C. Tell your partner about the following:

1. The most exotic food you have ever eaten.

2. A sacred place you have visited.

3. An ancient site that you would love to see.

4. A custom you have learned about in another country.

5. Something you avoid doing when you travel.

6. Your favourite tourist attraction in your home country.

MyBookshelf > My eLab > Exercises
> Unit 7 > Vocabulary

Build Your Knowledge

BEFORE YOU READ

A. Discuss this question with your class.

Imagine you are planning to visit a country, either for business or pleasure, that you have never been to before. What kinds of things do you think you will need to know?

GROUP READING: CUSTOMS AROUND THE WORLD

B. You are going to learn more about things to do, and not do, in various parts of the world. Work in groups of four. Student A reads Reading A; Student B reads Reading B; Student C reads Reading C; and Student D reads Reading D. Read attentively so you can explain the reading to your group members.

Reading A: Thailand

Thailand is an exotic country famous for its beautiful beaches, magnificent temples, ancient handicrafts, delicious food, and friendly people. Not surprisingly, Thailand is a popular vacation destination, but there are some cultural rules to follow when you visit the country.

When you visit a Thai temple, you must be careful to cover your body. Don't wear shorts or sleeveless shirts. You also need to take your shoes off in a temple. Look at how the local Thai people are behaving and follow their example.

Thailand has strict rules related to the human body. First, never touch anyone on the head. If you see a cute child, you must not pat him or her on the head. The head is considered sacred and cannot be touched. You also need to be careful with your feet. Never sit in such a way that the soles of your feet are visible; the feet are considered dirty, and sitting this way is impolite. You should also avoid pointing your feet directly at another person, for example, when you sit opposite someone. Avoid pointing your feet at Buddha statues, too.

© ERPI • Reproduction prohibited

Thailand is famous for its food; dishes such as Pad Thai and Tom Yum soup are well worth sampling. If you decide to try some Thai food, remember to eat with your spoon, not your fork. Use your fork to push the food onto your spoon.

You should also never say anything negative about the King of Thailand. Thais are patriotic people who take their monarchy very seriously. The national anthem is played publicly in the morning and evening; when you hear it, stop what you are doing and remain quiet.

Above all, stay calm, smile, and you won't go wrong!

Reading B: Mexico

The country of Mexico is known for its spectacular beaches, ancient ruins, and tropical climate. If you visit, either on business or as a tourist, here are some things to keep in mind.

Mexicans are warm, welcoming people. When Mexican women greet each other, they often kiss on the cheek. Men usually shake hands. People often stand closer together than those from North America, and casual touching is normal. If you back away, Mexicans will see this as rejection.

You need to understand the Mexican concept of time. If you plan to meet a Mexican friend or colleague, don't expect him to arrive on time—and don't be angry when he is late. Mexicans have a very flexible approach to time. If you are invited to dinner at someone's home, you should arrive at least thirty minutes later than the time of your invitation; if you arrive early, you will seem greedy.

If you are doing business in Mexico, remember that Mexicans often dress quite formally for work. Don't wear shorts or other clothes that you might wear to the beach. Remember, too, that Mexicans like to take a break in the afternoon (a "siesta"); if you try to conduct business during siesta time, you will be frustrated.

If you are invited to someone's home, it is a good idea to bring flowers—but don't bring red flowers, as Mexican folklore says they are used to cast spells. When you have finished your meal, it is polite to leave a small amount of food on the table; this shows that you have had plenty to eat. If you are given a gift, you should open it right away.

Be careful with your hands. In particular, you should understand that the "OK" sign, where the tip of your thumb touches the tip of your first finger to make a circle, is highly offensive.

Keep these tips in mind, and you will be warmly welcomed by your Mexican hosts.

Reading C: Morocco

As an Arab country and former French colony, Morocco is a delight for visitors. You can explore the country's rich history, bargain for treasures in the local markets, and even head out on a guided tour of the Sahara Desert. If you go to this North African country, remember the following tips.

Remember that this is an Arab country, and you need to respect Arab customs. You need to dress modestly: this means long skirts or pants and no bare shoulders. This is particularly the case in rural areas.

© ERPI • Reproduction prohibited

During the month of Ramadan, do not eat or drink in public as the local Islamic population will be observing this religious event and will not eat or drink anything during daylight hours.

If you are not Muslim, don't attempt to enter a mosque. Remember that these are religious sites, not tourist attractions. Don't stand outside a mosque trying to look inside or taking photographs of local people worshipping.

If you are invited to a Moroccan home, take a gift, such as flowers or fruit. When you arrive, always take your shoes off. You will sit around a low table, and there will typically be a large dish in the middle of the table. Everyone shares this dish. It is customary to use the right hand when eating. The left hand is reserved for bathroom tasks and cleaning, so if you can use your right hand, you should do so.

There are some conversation topics that are best avoided if you don't want to say the wrong thing. These include the royal family, the political situation in North Africa, and the use of drugs in Morocco.

Above all, be conservative and respectful, and you will have a wonderful adventure.

Reading D: Switzerland

When you think of Switzerland, you might think of mountains and skiing. You may enjoy Swiss chocolate or cheese. Or you might be more interested in banking. Whatever your reasons for travelling to Switzerland, remember these tips.

When you meet a Swiss person, remember that the Swiss can be quite formal with people they don't know well. Don't use a person's first name until you are invited to do so; use "Mr.," "Mrs.," or "Ms." Don't ask your new Swiss friend too many personal questions (such as questions about their income or religious beliefs), and don't tell a Swiss person all the details of your life until you know them better.

It is important in Switzerland to be on time for meetings and social events. If you are late, you will appear rude and disrespectful. If you go to someone's home, send a thank-you note the next day.

The Swiss do not like noise, so don't speak too loudly in public. If you are talking on your cell phone, don't shout. Stay in control of your emotions when other people are close by. When you are talking to someone, don't put your hands in your pockets or chew gum.

If you want to give someone a gift, don't choose anything too expensive. This will make a Swiss person think you want something from them. Never give anything sharp, such as a knife, as this symbolizes the end of the friendship. Good gifts are chocolates and flowers, but be careful with white flowers as these are used at funerals.

Above all, never throw garbage on the ground; the Swiss are proud of their beautiful country. Happy travels!

© ERPI • Reproduction prohibited

C. Take turns sharing your information with the rest of your group through a discussion. As you learn something about a country, add that piece of information to the country cards below. Ask each other questions to get the information you need.

Example: **Anna:** Here's something that I didn't know about Thailand. You shouldn't pat children on the head there.

Brian: Mexico has rules about hands, too. You shouldn't make the "OK" symbol.

Claire: And in Morocco, you should only use your right hand to eat. The left hand is associated with the bathroom, and with cleaning.

Daryl: Switzerland doesn't seem to have any customs around body parts. But you should make sure to be on time there!

Reading A

Culture Tips: Thailand
When visiting a temple: _____ _____
Head and feet: _____ _____
How to eat: _____ _____
Talking about the King: _____ _____
The national anthem: _____ _____

- Do you come from Thailand? If so, do you agree with the information given?

- If not, what surprised you most about what you have learned?

© ERPI • Reproduction prohibited

Reading B

Culture Tips: Mexico
How to greet people:
Personal space:
When to arrive:
Siesta time:
Hand gestures:

- Do you come from Mexico? If so, do you agree with the information given?
- If not, what surprised you most about what you have learned?

Reading C

Culture Tips: Morocco
How to dress:
Ramadan:
Visiting mosques:
Visiting homes:
How to eat:
Conversation:

© ERPI • Reproduction prohibited

- Do you come from Morocco? If so, do you agree with the information given?
- If not, what surprised you most about what you have learned?

Reading D

Culture Tips: Switzerland
How to address people:
Conversation:
Arriving on time:
Noise levels:
Gifts:
Littering:

- Do you come from Switzerland? If so, do you agree with the information given?
- If not, what surprised you most about what you have learned?

MyBookshelf > My eLab > Exercises
> Unit 7 > Customs around the World

© ERPI • Reproduction prohibited

Share Your Ideas

With your group, discuss the following questions.

1. What country has a custom that is very similar to something in your country? Describe the custom and explain how it similar to your own custom.

2. What country has a custom that is the exact opposite, or very different from, your country? In what ways is the custom different?

3. What is a custom you read about that really surprised you? Why were you surprised?

4. What is a custom from your country that you think might surprise people from elsewhere? Why?

5. Based on what you've read and heard, have any of these customs influenced your feelings about visiting these countries? Explain your answer to your group.

Develop Speaking Fluency: Work in Groups 1
Work Together to Solve a Problem

In your studies and in your career, you need to work in groups. In college or university, you may be assigned a long-term project in which you carry out an experiment or do research in the library or in your community. You will write up your results together in a formal report, or make a joint presentation, or both, and in many cases, you will all get the same grade. In the workplace, you will often have to work in groups; this is particularly true in business careers and in health care.

It is important to be prepared for this, and to develop an understanding of how groups function and what the role of each participant is.

DO YOU ENJOY GROUP WORK?

A. Work in pairs. Discuss these questions.

1. Do you like working on group projects or assignments? Why, or why not?

2. What is the value of group projects or assignments?

3. Can you think of any groups or teams that have many talented members but that don't function well as a group? You might, for example, think of a sports team. Why do you think this group cannot achieve success?

© ERPI • Reproduction prohibited

GROUP ROLES

In 1948, Kenneth D. Benne and Paul Sheats came up with twenty-six different roles that people might play in groups. Although their work is over seventy years old, it is still considered a very good summary of the different approaches that individuals can take to group work. Some of the most common roles are listed below.

B. Work in pairs. Decide what each person might say. The first is done for you.

Role		Possible Response
1. Initiator *Suggests new ideas*	d	**a)** "I think that might work well. My main concern is …"
2. Information Giver *Provides details*		**b)** "That's a terrible idea. I can't believe you said that."
3. Opinion Giver *Provides opinions*		**c)** "I think we can reach a compromise here."
4. Coordinator *Organizes the group's activities*		**d)** "I've just had a great idea! Why don't we …"
5. Energizer *Prods the group to decide*		**e)** "First, we'll do some research. Next, we'll work in pairs."
6. Dominator *Wants to be in control*		**f)** "Ian, Liz, what do you both think? Which solution do you like best?"
7. Harmonizer *Deals with disagreements*		**g)** "I've just researched this, and I've found out that …"
8. Gatekeeper *Encourages everyone to participate*		**h)** "We need to reach a decision. We don't have much time to spare."
9. Recorder *Keeps a record of activities*		**i)** "Listen to me. I know best."
10. Aggressor *Attacks the work of others*		**j)** "I'll make a note of that."

C. With your partner, discuss these questions.

1. Which of the roles listed above do you think are positive? Which are negative?

2. Can you think of group experiences you have had, in which individuals played some of these roles?

3. Do you recognize yourself in any of these roles? Which role(s) have you played in various groups?

© ERPI • Reproduction prohibited

D. Work in pairs. For each of the strategies listed below, select two pieces of useful language from the box.

> • Do any of us have a special skill that we can use?
> • Is everyone sure about what we need to do?
> • I think we need to talk about why we can't agree.
> • I think that's a good idea, but there might be another possibility.
> • Let's make sure we understand the instructions before we start.
> • We don't have much time, so let's get started.
> • It's important that we all put the same amount of work into this.
> • What do you think is the best way to divide up the work?
> • Can we help you to become more involved with the project?
> • I think we have some great ideas here—this is really good teamwork.
> • Good thoughts, but I wonder if we should also consider …?
> • There is a lot to do, so let's try to stay focused.

1. Find out exactly what is expected of you and your group. What does your project entail? Will you get a grade for the assignment, and will everyone get the same grade? If this is not clear, check with your instructor.

_____

_____

2. Find out which strengths each member has. Is there someone who has strong research skills? Let that person do library research. Is there someone who has strong design skills? Maybe that person can be in charge of designing the presentation you will give.

_____

_____

3. Respect each other. It is important that all members feel that their contribution is valued. If you disagree with someone, do so respectfully and politely. Don't criticize others.

_____

_____

4. Pace yourself, and make sure you all stay on track. You have a limited amount of time, so don't get distracted. Don't get into a situation where you are scrambling at the end to make sure everything gets done on time.

_____

_____

© **ERPI** • Reproduction prohibited

5. Try to ensure that everyone does the same amount of work. If someone is not doing his share of the work, it's important to find out why. It's important to be honest about such issues, and to work together to help the group member to play his or her role in the project.

_____

_____

6. Keep the atmosphere positive and optimistic. If there is conflict in the group, deal with it immediately. Don't ignore a problem in the hope that it will get better; it won't.

_____

_____

MyBookshelf > My eLab > Exercises
> Unit 7 > Strategies

■ Improve Your Pronunciation: Linking Words

A. Say this sentence: Chefs in Egypt will be upset if you put salt on your food.

How did you pronounce these words? In many cases, the last sound in a word is joined in speech to the first sound in the following word. For example:

Chefs in ⟶ Chefs in

upset if ⟶ upset if

salt on ⟶ salt on

In fluent speech, this kind of linking is very common.

B. Work in pairs. Look at these sentences and decide which sounds can be linked. Draw a linking symbol ‿ to show the joined words.

1. If you visit a Thai temple, remember to take your shoes off. Don't touch anyone on the head.

2. Erica works for an international company in Ontario. She lives in Ottawa but often goes away to visit her family in Atlanta.

3. Pedro stayed in a village in the Swiss Alps. He enjoyed eating Swiss food, such as chocolate.

4. Danielle wanted to have an adventure. She visited Antarctica and saw penguins and other birds.

5. Don't take photos of people who stand outside mosques in Arab countries. This is not polite.

6. Johnny eats at an outdoor market in Athens every night instead of cooking.

7. Mexicans are warm and outgoing people. Women greet each other with a kiss on the cheek.

C. Listen to the sentences. Repeat each one.

MyBookshelf > My eLab > Exercises
> Unit 7 > Pronunciation

© **ERPI** • Reproduction prohibited

Bring It All Together

A. Read the following email from the administrators of your language program to all students.

Re: Culture Day
To: Students

Date: May 1, 2019

We have decided to hold a special event at the end of term—a Culture Day! Our goal is to help students to learn about different parts of the world and to become familiar with different customs and expectations for behaviour. For an entire day, you will learn about other countries through a variety of activities.

What kinds of activities? That's up to you, but the day could include lectures, discussion groups, workshops on traditional handicrafts, language lessons, singing and dancing, cooking lessons, and much more. We expect the day will end with a multicultural dinner.

We are asking all students to come up with a plan for what the day should look like. Think about what would help you most to learn about the world. You can also think about how you might want to share your own country's culture with other students. The group with the best plan will work together with the administration to put their ideas into practice.

We have a reasonable budget for this event, but don't go overboard! Buying special food items is certainly possible. Buying tickets to fly you all to the country of your dreams is not!

B. Work in groups of three or four to plan a Culture Day for your language program. Your plan should address the following questions. Use the language presented on page 91. Make your notes on a separate page. Remember to be as detailed as possible.

1. What are your goals for the event? What do you hope to learn from it? Are you going to focus on one specific country, or will you explore the culture of several?

2. Where will the event be held? Will you use your classrooms, will you use another room in your school or college, or will you rent a different place? If you decide to go somewhere else, how much will it cost?

3. Who are you going to invite—only the students from your language program, or other guests? If the event is open to other guests, how will you promote it? How many people do you expect to be there?

4. What activities are you going to have: talks, hands-on workshops, lessons? What will these be about? Will participants have a choice of activities?

5. Who will lead the activities? Will you bring in guest speakers? Where will you find these people? Will you need to pay them? If so, how much?

6. What will the dinner be like? Which food are you going to present? Who will cook it? What will it cost to buy the ingredients?

7. How are you going to manage large numbers of people? What will you need to do to ensure that no one gets lost and that everyone has a good time?

8. What is your total budget? If your planned activities are too expensive, where can you save money?

© ERPI • Reproduction prohibited

C. Share your ideas with your class. Take a vote on which group has the best plan.

D. Think about your own performance in the group. Which of the roles on page 90 did you play? Which roles did you see other members of your group playing? Discuss these questions with your group.

HOW DID YOU DO?

Did your group apply the strategies you have learned in this unit? Fill in the chart below to evaluate your own performance in this activity.

Strategy	Did we do this?		
	Yes	I'm not sure ...	No
We all played positive, supportive roles in the group.			
We understood what we were expected to do.			
We used each member's strengths successfully.			
We were respectful and avoided harsh criticism.			
We avoided distractions and stayed focused.			
All members made an equal contribution.			
We maintained a positive and optimistic outlook.			

Go Further

Cassandra (Cassie) De Pecol is an American explorer of countries and cultures.

A. Work in groups of three or four. Use the Internet to answer the following questions.

1. What world records does Cassie hold?

_____

_____

_____

2. Why did Cassie decide to pursue this goal?

_____

_____

© ERPI • Reproduction prohibited

3. How did she pay for her travels?

_____

_____

4. How long did she stay in each country? What did she do there?

_____

_____

5. Find information about one country Cassie visited. What did she learn about this country?

_____

_____

B. In your groups, discuss the following questions.

1. Cassie calls herself a "traveller" and "explorer." How is this different from being a "tourist"?

2. Cassie spent between two and five days in each country. Some people say this is not enough; she did not learn anything about the culture in such a short time. Are short visits a waste of time? Why, or why not?

3. During her travels, Cassie served as an ambassador for an organization called the International Institute of Peace through Tourism. What do you think is the connection between tourism and peace?

© ERPI • Reproduction prohibited

UNIT 8

In this unit, you will learn to do the following:

Think critically about the impact of green space.

Use vocabulary related to environmental concerns.

Learn about the importance of creativity.

Learn strategies to develop creativity.

Take part in a group activity requiring creative thought.

Distinguish between /i:/ and /ɪ/ sounds

URBAN GREEN SPACES

Discuss the Topic

A. Work in pairs. Discuss the following questions.

1. Which of the following activities do you enjoy in a park? Check all the activities you enjoy.

   ☐ meeting friends   ☐ walking   ☐ relaxing

   ☐ games or activities   ☐ photography/painting   ☐ watching nature

   ☐ other _____   ☐ I never go to a park.

2. Do you come from a big city, a medium-sized city, a small city, or a more rural area?

   _____

3. What kinds of parks and green spaces do you have where you live?

   _____

4. How often do you visit parks and green spaces?

   _____

5. Do you tend to meet friends there, or is it something you do on your own?

   _____

B. What is your favourite park to spend time in? Share your thoughts with your class.

Develop Your Vocabulary

A. Work in pairs. Write each word under one of the pictures below. Use each word only once.

urban green space | redevelopment | composting | recycling
urban renewal | carbon dioxide | habitat | wetland

1. _____   2. _____

© ERPI • Reproduction prohibited

3. _____

4. _____

5. _____

6. _____

7. _____

8. _____

B. Tell your partner about the following:

1. The most famous park in your country.

2. Reasons why people go to that park.

3. A park you have heard about in another country.

© **ERPI** • Reproduction prohibited

4. Why this park is considered famous.

5. Other green spaces that aren't actually parks in your city.

6. Somewhere you visited because it was natural.

MyBookshelf > My eLab > Exercises
> Unit 8 > Vocabulary

Build Your Knowledge

BEFORE YOU WATCH

A. Discuss these questions with your class.

1. Why is New York City's Central Park so famous?

2. Have you ever been to Central Park? Have you seen it in a movie or TV show?

3. What do you suppose people like to do there?

VIDEO: URBAN PARKS: GOOD FOR THE CITY AND THE ENVIRONMENT

B. Watch the video. In this video, you will be taken on a tour of Central Park in New York by Professor Bill Chameides of Duke University to learn more about why urban green spaces are important.

AFTER YOU WATCH

C. Work in pairs. Answer these questions.

1. What are some reasons green spaces are good for the city's environment?

_____

_____

2. What are some benefits of parks for big cities?

_____

_____

3. What are some specific benefits of trees for the environment?

_____

_____

© **ERPI** • Reproduction prohibited

4. What are some good things about the lakes in Central Park?

_____

_____

5. What is notable about the size of Central Park?

_____

_____

6. What are some of the attractions in Central Park?

_____

_____

7. What benefits of Central Park would also be true of other urban parks?

_____

_____

MyBookshelf > My eLab > Exercises
> Unit 8 > Urban Parks

Share Your Ideas

Join another pair to make a group of four. With your group, discuss the following questions.

1. What is the most important thing you have learned from this video?

2. Think about a park that you know. Does any of Dr. Chameides's information about Central Park apply to your park? How is your park similar? How is it different? Complete the chart.

	_____'s park	_____'s park	_____'s park	_____'s park
Similarities to Central Park				
Differences from Central Park				

3. "As the world changes and cities grow, parks are going to be more important than ever." Do you agree? In what ways do you think parks will become more important?

© ERPI • Reproduction prohibited

4. Dr. Chameides suggests that if you don't have a green space where you live, you can talk to local politicians. How interested in green spaces do you think your local politicians are? Mark a point on the line, then discuss your thoughts with your group.

←——————————————————————————————→

**Very interested. In my
city, we think this is
very important.**

**Not at all interested.
Empty space is used
for building, not parks.**

5. If you could design a park from the beginning, what would it have?

Develop Speaking Fluency: Work in Groups 2
Find Creative Solutions

In many areas of study, and in many professions, creativity is rewarded. College and university instructors appreciate students who come up with creative solutions to problems. Employers do, too. Finding creative solutions to problems is sometimes called "thinking outside the box." This is a great skill to cultivate as you prepare for further studies or develop your career.

HOW CREATIVE ARE YOU?

A. Work in pairs. Discuss these questions.

1. Do you consider yourself creative? Why, or why not?

2. Think of a time in your studies or in your job when you needed to find a creative solution to a problem. What happened?

3. Do you think some people are naturally creative, or do you think anyone can learn to be creative? Explain your answer to your partner.

BE A CREATIVE THINKER

B. Niko has recently started his own website design business. Read Niko's social media post and the responses he has received on the next page. On your own, rank them in order from most helpful to least helpful.

		Name of respondent
Most helpful	1.	
	2.	
	3.	
	4.	
	5.	
	6.	
	7.	
Least helpful	8.	

© ERPI • Reproduction prohibited

Niko
@Niko

9:27 PM – May 20, 2019

Problem! Need to design a really cool and original website for client's gardening business. No idea what to do. Not feeling very creative today. Need to get the creative juices flowing—but how? #becreative

FOLLOW

Michelle   12 min
@Michelle

Talk to people and share your ideas. The best way to develop good ideas is through discussion with your colleagues and friends. Plant a small idea, talk about it, and let it grow—just like a garden! ☺

Warren   16 min
@Warren

Don't stare at the computer screen waiting for inspiration to appear out of nowhere. It won't. Get up and do something physical—cook dinner, go for a walk, wash the car. There's something about physical activity that inspires creativity.

Rosalind   22 min
@Rosalind

There are no original ideas any more. Look at some other gardening websites, and see what ideas you like best. See if you can borrow someone else's ideas and make them look like your own.

Derek   37 min
@Derek

I'm a teacher, and I always teach my students to be creative by getting them to draw things. Take a piece of paper and a pencil, and sketch what you think the website should look like. Or come up with a basic idea and use a mind map to see what you can add to it!

Erica   39 min
@Erica

Sleep on it! The perfect idea might come to you in your dreams.

Rudy   48 min
@Rudy

Educate yourself about the topic. Go and visit some gardens. Go to the park and the botanical garden, and see what you like. Use the plants and garden designs that appeal to you as inspiration for your work.

Betsy   1 h
@Betsy

Think big! Imagine the perfect website. Does it have music? Animations? What can you do to make this happen? Don't say you can't do it, or you don't have the technology. Dream big, and you can scale it back later if you need to.

Harvey   1h10
@Harvey

Have you tried meditation or yoga? They will help to clear your mind and make you more focused on the task. They always work for me!

© **ERPI** • Reproduction prohibited

With your partner, discuss these questions.

1. Which advice did you think was most helpful? Which advice would you follow? Which would be less helpful for you? Why?

2. Have you ever been in a situation like Niko, where you needed to be creative? What did you do?

3. Can you think of any other advice that Niko's friends didn't give him?

STRATEGIES FOR MAKING AND RESPONDING TO CREATIVE SOLUTIONS

Some of the best ideas start out as a small idea, which grows as people discuss the idea with others.

If you have an idea, never be afraid to share it with your classmates. Even if your idea is not practical, is too expensive, or is otherwise unrealistic, don't hesitate to share it. You may be able to work with it and develop it into something that is more manageable.

If someone offers a creative idea, encourage that person. Don't immediately tell the person the idea is not possible. Be supportive. See if you can help the person to reach a solution that might work well.

D. Work in pairs. Look at the following ways to suggest a creative idea or a solution to a problem. Decide whether each response is positive (P) or negative (N).

Suggestions: I have a great idea!

I've been thinking about this problem, and I think …

One possibility might be …

We could think about …

Responses: _____ I think that's a great idea.

_____ I wonder if that's possible …

_____ Hmmm … it may be too expensive.

_____ That could be a really good solution.

_____ It sounds great, but would it work in practice?

_____ I don't think _____ would agree to it.

_____ It's an interesting idea, but …

_____ That's a really unique approach to the problem.

≥ **E. With your partner, take turns playing the roles of Student A and Student B. Keep each discussion going as long as you can—use your imagination!**

1. Student A: You think your school should plant a vegetable garden on the roof.

Student B: You think the money could be better spent on other things, like new books.

2. Student A: You want to get a summer job planting trees in a remote region.

Student B: You think it's a waste of time, and Student B could make more money in the city.

3. Student A: You think the cafeteria should ask students to separate food waste for composting.

Student B: You think that would be very inconvenient and no one will do it.

4. Student A: You think your school should remove its vending machines to create less waste.

Student B: You think students will just bring drinks and snacks from outside.

MyBookshelf > My eLab > Exercises
> Unit 8 > Strategies

■ Improve Your Pronunciation: Sounds /iː/ and /ɪ/

A. Say this sentence: It isn't easy to live a green lifestyle.

Some of the words in this sentence have a long *i* (the sound in the word *green*), and some have a short *i* (the sound in *live*). The long *i* is common in many languages, but not all languages have the short *i*.

B. Listen to the words. Do you hear a long *i* /iː/ or a short *i* /ɪ/?

1. Long *i* /iː/	Short *i* /ɪ/	**7.** Long *i* /iː/	Short *i* /ɪ/
2. Long *i* /iː/	Short *i* /ɪ/	**8.** Long *i* /iː/	Short *i* /ɪ/
3. Long *i* /iː/	Short *i* /ɪ/	**9.** Long *i* /iː/	Short *i* /ɪ/
4. Long *i* /iː/	Short *i* /ɪ/	**10.** Long *i* /iː/	Short *i* /ɪ/
5. Long *i* /iː/	Short *i* /ɪ/	**11.** Long *i* /iː/	Short *i* /ɪ/
6. Long *i* /iː/	Short *i* /ɪ/	**12.** Long *i* /iː/	Short *i* /ɪ/

C. Practise these sounds by playing a game. Follow these instructions:

1. Divide into two teams.

2. A player from Team A chooses a word from the list below. The player gives a definition of the word without saying the word. Example: *It's part of your mouth.*

3. A player from Team B must guess the word. The player pronounces the word with the correct pronunciation.

4. Your teacher will decide whether the correct sound has been used. If the pronunciation is correct, Team B gets a point. If not, no points are given.

5. Repeat, with different members of each team choosing and defining words.

rich	reach	bin	bean	green	grin	fist	feast
sleep	slip	tin	teen	knit	neat	skim	scheme
ship	sheep	lip	leap	dip	deep	pill	peel

© ERPI • Reproduction prohibited

D. Listen and repeat each word.

MyBookshelf > My eLab > Exercises
> Unit 8 > Pronunciation

Bring It All Together

A. Read the following newspaper item.

DISUSED INDUSTRIAL SPACE TO BECOME URBAN GREEN SPACE

Plans are underway to redevelop a disused industrial wasteland on Oak Street. The site once held factories and warehouses, but it has been abandoned for several years now. The derelict buildings have already been demolished. The site, which is surrounded on three sides by office buildings and high-rise apartment buildings, will be turned into a green space for residents and office workers.

B. Work in groups of three or four to design a plan for the space where the parking garage stood.

Things you need to know:

- The space is in the downtown core of a large urban centre. There is no other green space within four kilometres. The city has a large park on the banks of a river, but it isn't within easy walking distance.

- The city has warm summers and cool, rainy winters. There is very little snow, and the region is not affected by extreme weather conditions like hurricanes or tornadoes.

- The area surrounding the space was neglected, but it is now experiencing a period of renewal. There are many long-term residents in the apartment buildings to the north, including a large number of seniors, but young families are also moving in. However, the neighbourhood still has a high rate of drug abuse, and there is some crime.

- The only way to access the site is from Oak Street, which is a very busy street with a wide variety of stores and restaurants.

Things you should talk about:

- Who will be the main users of the space? What will they want to see and do? Discuss which of the following you want to include: a playground, picnic tables, a swimming pool, a pond, washroom facilities, outdoor seating, sculptures, or other forms of outdoor art, food stands, a space for dogs, a space for musicians to play, a weekly farmers' market, or something else.

- What are you going to plant in the space? Will you plant trees for shade? Will you have mostly grass, will there be walking trails, or will parts of the space be paved? How about flowers? Will the space have a theme, such as modern, traditional, Asian-inspired, or family-friendly?

- Are you going to encourage the presence of wildlife, such as birds, frogs, fish, or other creatures? If so, how?

© ERPI • Reproduction prohibited

- What can you do to keep children safe, considering that Oak Street is a very busy street?

- What rules should be in place for the use of the park? Will it close at a certain time? Will dogs be allowed? How about cyclists and inline skaters? How can you ensure that the space isn't used by criminals, such as drug dealers, especially at night?

C. Design your urban green space below. Remember to be as detailed as possible.

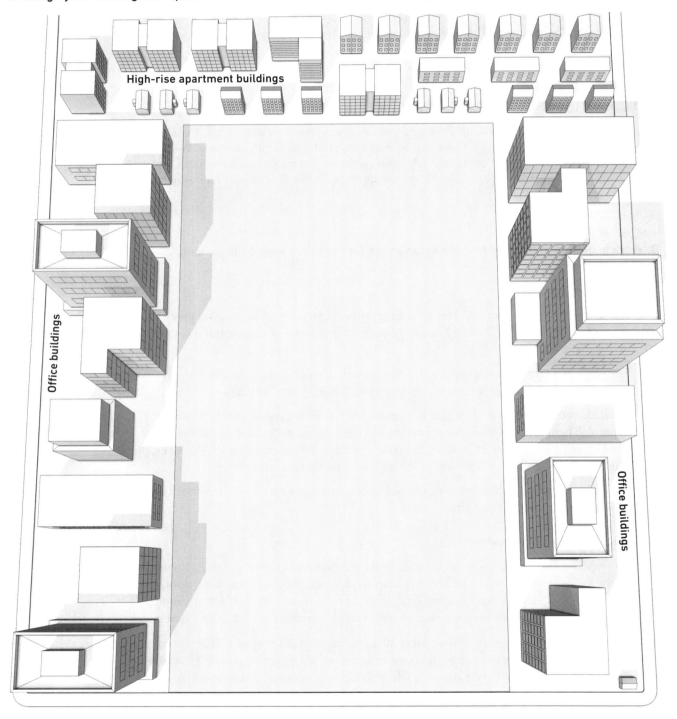

High-rise apartment buildings

Office buildings

Office buildings

Oak Street

© **ERPI** • Reproduction prohibited

USEFUL PHRASES

Make a suggestion.

I have a great idea!

I've been thinking about this problem, and I think ...

One possibility might be ...

We could think about ...

Respond positively.

I think that's a great idea.

That could be a really good solution.

That's a really unique approach to the problem.

Express concern.

I wonder if that's possible ...

Hmmm ... it may be too expensive.

It sounds great, but would it work in practice?

I don't think _____ would agree to it.

It's an interesting idea, but ...

D. Share your ideas with your class in the form of a short presentation. Take a vote on which group has the best design.

HOW DID YOU DO?

Did your group apply the strategies you have learned in this unit? Fill in the chart below to evaluate your own performance in this activity.

Strategy	Did we do this?		
	Yes	I'm not sure ...	No
We all played positive, supportive roles in the group.			
We encouraged each other to offer creative ideas.			
We used appropriate language to respond to each other's ideas.			
We shared ideas and came up with solutions that we were happy with.			
We were respectful and avoided harsh criticism.			

© **ERPI** • Reproduction prohibited

Go Further

This is the Queen Elizabeth Olympic Park in London, England.

The park was created for the 2012 Olympic Games.

A. Work in groups of three or four. Use the Internet to answer the following questions.

1. What was in this space before it was turned into the Olympic Park?

_____

_____

2. What role did this park play during the 2012 Olympic Games?

_____

_____

3. What is the ArcelorMittal Orbit? What record does it hold?

_____

_____

4. In what ways has the park protected the environment?

_____

_____

5. Since the end of the Olympic games, several educational and cultural organizations have established, or are planning to establish, centres within the Park. Name some.

_____

_____

B. In your groups, discuss the following questions.

1. Do you know of any other old Olympic sites? What are they now used for?

2. The Queen Elizabeth Olympic Park was once in a depressed part of London. Can you think of any areas in your city or your country that have been improved through the development of old industrial space?

3. What might prevent the development of new parks in your city?

© ERPI • Reproduction prohibited

In this unit, you will learn to do the following:

Think critically about issues in the workplace.

Use vocabulary related to feelings about work.

Learn to design an effective poster.

Work in a group to find a solution to a problem.

Present your ideas in the form of a poster presentation.

Use reduced speech to make your speech more fluent.

ALL IN A DAY'S WORK

Discuss the Topic

A. Do you have a job? Have you had a job in the past, or do you plan to have one in the future? What factors are important for you when choosing a job? Complete the table on your own. Then, discuss your answers with a partner.

1: Very important
2: Somewhat important
3: Not sure
4: Not very important
5: Not at all important

Factors when choosing a job	1	2	3	4	5
1. Making a lot of money					
2. Having several weeks' vacation each year					
3. Being respected in your community					
4. Being a boss or team leader					
5. Being able to set your own schedule					
6. Being able to work from home					
7. Being part of a large, friendly team					
8. Using your creative talents					
9. Working to make other people's lives better					
10. Travelling for your work					
11. Having perks, such as gym memberships					
12. Working a regular Monday–Friday schedule					
13. Working outdoors in nature					
14. Having a lot of variety in your work					
15. Having opportunities to learn new skills					
16. Having a comfortable office					
17. Having access to free further education					
18. Not needing to take work home at night					

B. Which were the most important factors in your class? Which were the least important? Discuss these questions with your class.

© **ERPI** • Reproduction prohibited

Develop Your Vocabulary

A. Work in pairs. Read the sentences below. For each word in bold, decide which sentence gives the same meaning.

1. I'm **overwhelmed**. I have to finish three reports before I go home tonight, and I have to prepare for a meeting with my boss tomorrow morning.
   a) I have too much work.
   b) I'm bored by my work.

2. Marissa didn't get the job she wanted. She is feeling **discouraged** about her career.
   a) She isn't qualified for the job she wanted.
   b) She doesn't think she will ever have a successful career.

3. Jordan is **motivated** by his new job in a software development company. He wants to do well.
   a) He's excited by his job.
   b) He's stressed by his job.

4. Lina's boss keeps changing her mind about when employees can take vacation time. Lina is **confused** about what to do.
   a) She's uncertain about what to do.
   b) She's annoyed with her boss.

5. With his advanced software training, Charlie is **optimistic** that he will be offered a promotion.
   a) He's excited about doing well in his current job.
   b) He has a positive feeling about getting a better job in the future.

6. Our photocopier keeps breaking down. We're all really **frustrated**!
   a) We're getting a little angry.
   b) We're happy that we have good equipment.

7. I love my new job. I'm never bored, and I'm feeling really **challenged**.
   a) I'm making plenty of money in my new job.
   b) I'm learning a lot in my new job.

8. The workers were **enthusiastic** about the new schedule.
   a) They reacted positively to the new schedule.
   b) They had some concerns about the new schedule.

9. Tatiana has been working seventy hours a week at the same job for over a year, and she has not taken a vacation for eighteen months. No wonder she feels **burned out**!
   a) She's feeling very positive about her job.
   b) She's tired from working so hard.

10. Nicholas is **inspired** by the people in his office. They are so creative and forward-thinking.
    a) He feels concerned because he isn't as good as they are.
    b) He admires them, and he wants to be as good as they are.

© ERPI • Reproduction prohibited

B. Which of the underlined words and phrases have a positive meaning? Which have a negative meaning?

Positive: _____

Negative: _____

C. Tell your partner about the following:

1. A time you felt frustrated in a job.

2. A career you are enthusiastic about.

3. A time when you felt overwhelmed by your responsibilities.

4. Something you are optimistic about.

5. A task that makes you feel challenged.

6. A time when you felt motivated to succeed.

MyBookshelf > My eLab > Exercises
> Unit 9 > Vocabulary

Build Your Knowledge

BEFORE YOU READ

A. Discuss these questions with your class.

1. Do you have a job, or have you ever had one? How does/did the job make you feel?

2. Which careers do you think are especially stressful?

3. What are some good ways to deal with stress in the workplace?

READING: THE WORKING WORLD

B. Work in pairs. Read the stories of seven different working people. After you have read them, choose the word that best describes each person.

challenged | burned out | frustrated | optimistic | confused | overwhelmed | inspired

Arlene, 26

1. I started a new job as a sales representative for a pharmaceutical company two months ago. The work is fine, and I am learning a lot, but I keep getting mixed messages about my salary and benefits. My first paycheque was smaller than I had expected. I was also told that I would be given a company car and a gym membership. There has been no sign of those things. I know I have health insurance, but I don't know exactly what it covers. I'm not sure if I can go to the dentist or get new glasses. I work for two supervisors, and they tell me two different things. I don't know who to believe.

She is _____. confused

© ERPI • Reproduction prohibited

Dale, 23

2. I work in public relations for a local theatre company. It's my first job since I graduated from college. I've been with the company for a year now, and I've just gotten a really positive performance review from my supervisor. Everyone says they're happy with my work. I've made some good contacts for the company, and I know I've represented them well. They say they really value what I'm doing, and they've given me a small raise. I like my job, but I think I might look for a new position in a bigger organization; I know I have a great future ahead of me.

He is _____. *challenged*

Emilia, 45

3. I still remember the first day I spent working as part of an ambulance crew. I felt so excited and so proud. I really wanted to be able to help people. But I work such long hours, and I'm under a lot of stress in my job. I think it's having an effect on me, both physically and mentally. I'm completely exhausted when I finish a shift. My head aches, my back hurts, and I can't concentrate on anything. I get angry and upset very easily, too. My family doesn't have much money, so I haven't had a vacation in over three years. I sometimes wonder how much longer I can keep going out on emergency calls. *burned out*

She is _____.

Marek, 24

4. I'm training to be a teacher, and my course of study requires several placements in a classroom. I'm currently doing my first placement. I was told I would be actually working with students in the classroom, but when I got here, the teacher told me to sit in her office and correct papers all day. I've been here two weeks, and I hardly ever go into the classroom, except to sing the national anthem in the morning! Most of the time, the teacher shows videos to the class or plays on her computer. The students do nothing, and I sit in the office and correct papers. This is a waste of my time. I'm not learning anything! *frustrated*

He is _____.

Serena, 25

5. I'm a fashion designer in my first job. I've always loved clothes, so this is a great career for me. I think I'm good at creating outfits, but you should see some of the designs that my colleagues Ray and Dana produce! Their work is incredible—such a great use of colour and shape. They make me want to work as hard as I can to be as good as them. Of course, I don't want to copy their designs—I want to explore my own ideas—but they bring out the best in me!

She is _____. *inspired*

© **ERPI** • Reproduction prohibited

Boris, 34

6. I've just started a new job as a real estate agent. This is a second career for me; I worked in telemarketing before, but I didn't make enough money. There is certainly a lot to learn here. I have to learn marketing techniques, customer service strategies, and property law. Above all, I have to know how to close a sale. It sounds overwhelming, but it isn't, really. It's interesting to learn all this, and I'm enjoying developing my skills. I don't think I'll be bored in this career!

He is _____.   *opt*

Annabeth, 29

7. I'm an administrative assistant for a magazine publisher. The economy is weak at the moment, and the company is trying to save money to avoid going bankrupt. One of their solutions is to cut the number of administrative assistants in half. Six months ago, I worked for two vice-presidents; now I work for four of them! I cannot keep up with how much work I have to do. I come to work early every day, I stay late, and I even take work home with me, but I just can't do it. There's enough work for at least two people, if not three, but I'm the only one trying to do it! I need someone to help me.

She is _____.   *over whelmed*

AFTER YOU READ

C. Now, with your partner, decide which person is being discussed by his or her co-worker.

Arlene | Dale | Emilia | Marek | Serena | Boris | Annabeth

1. She's new to this kind of work, and she hasn't shown much imagination yet. That's okay—if she spends more time watching us at work, she'll learn to take chances. We're pretty creative.

_____

2. He is good at his job and has a great future ahead of him. I just hope we can persuade him to stay here. We can't pay much, but we do appreciate his work.

_____

3. My new administrative assistant is so slow! I don't understand what the problem is. It isn't that hard to write an email or make a phone call. I miss the assistant I used to have.

_____

4. I don't know what's wrong with her. She looks tired, and she's been very tense recently. She snapped at me the other day when I said "Good morning" to her. Maybe she needs a vacation.

_____

© ERPI • Reproduction prohibited

5. Student teachers need to be more involved, not just sit in an office. He needs to speak up and make his feelings known. If he doesn't do that, people will think he's bored. He won't get a good evaluation.

_____

6. He's making a good impression so far. He's very enthusiastic, and he even seems to enjoy the boring parts of the job, like paperwork. There is a lot to learn, but he's doing well.

_____

7. She keeps asking questions about cars, dentists, gym memberships—things that have nothing to do with her work. I wish she would focus on her job a little more.

_____

MyBookshelf > My eLab > Exercises
> Unit 9 > The Working World

Share Your Ideas

Join another pair to make a group of four. With your group, discuss the following questions.

1. Which of the people described in Build Your Knowledge
   a) do you admire most?
   b) do you sympathize with? Why?

2. Do you know anyone who has experienced negative feelings in connection with their jobs? What did they do about it?

3. In many countries, it is becoming less common for someone to stay in the same job (and even the same career) for his or her entire career.
   a) Do you expect to stay in the same career for your entire working life? Why, or why not?
   b) Can you imagine having several careers? If so, what might they be?

4. Look at these two points of view:

> Opinion A: Technology has made jobs much easier now. The workplace has changed for the better.

> Opinion B: The negative effects of technology on the workplace outweigh the positive effects. The workplace is changing for the worse.

© ERPI • Reproduction prohibited

For each point of view, think of three reasons why the speaker might have this opinion. Complete the chart with your ideas. Which opinion do you most agree with?

	Opinion A	Opinion B
Reason 1		
Reason 2		
Reason 3		

5. Did you receive any career counselling in school? If so, did you follow the advice of the counsellor? Why, or why not?

Develop Speaking Fluency: Work in Groups 3
Share Your Ideas: The Poster Presentation

One way to share the results of your group activities is through a poster presentation. Many courses at college and university ask students to work in pairs or groups to design a poster presentation about an aspect of their studies. Typically, posters are displayed on the wall. This may happen at your college or university; a poster display is also a common feature of many academic and professional conferences.

An effective poster contains some text (often in point form) along with photographs, charts, graphs, and other forms of visual representation of ideas.

The presenter stands next to the poster and summarizes the information on the poster and answers questions from people who stop to look at the poster.

Giving an effective poster presentation has two steps: (a) designing the poster; and (b) talking to people who stop to look at the poster.

© **ERPI** • Reproduction prohibited

STRATEGIES FOR DESIGNING YOUR POSTER

You can use computer software, such as PowerPoint, to design your poster, or you can make a very effective poster with poster card and cut-out images.

A. Work in pairs. Look at the poster on this page. This is a good example of an effective poster. With your partner, discuss what you like about this poster.

B. With your partner, decide what you should do when you design a poster. Underline the correct information.

1. Include **as much information as possible** / **the key points** on your poster.

2. Have a clear title at the **top** / **bottom** of your poster. Add your name, contact information, and any references you used.

3. Display your material in a **logical** / **random** design.

4. Use **many different** / **a few key** colours.

5. Keep your written information large enough: aim for a font size of **12 pt.** / **20 pt.** or more.

6. Write your text in **paragraphs** / **bullet points**.

7. **Use pictures and diagrams on your poster.** / **Fill the entire poster with written information.**

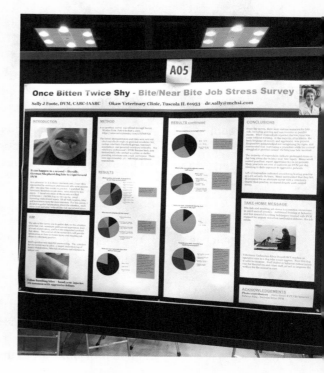

C. Work in pairs. Find some examples of posters on the Internet. Evaluate each one and discuss its strengths and weaknesses. What do you like? What do you think could be improved? Complete the table.

Source or URL	Topic of poster	Strengths	Weaknesses

© ERPI • Reproduction prohibited

GIVING THE POSTER PRESENTATION

Giving a poster presentation is not the same as giving a presentation to your class.

D. Work in pairs. Complete the table to show how giving a poster presentation is different from a class presentation.

	Class presentation	Poster presentation
Room	You are the only presenter in the room. Everyone is looking at you. The room should be quiet.	_____
Audience	You are presenting to a group of people.	_____
Time	There is a clear start time and end time. Your talk lasts for a set amount of time, for example, ten minutes.	_____
Format	You speak, and your audience members listen. Any questions are usually asked at the end.	_____
Preparation	You know in advance exactly what you want to say, and the order in which you want to say it. You do not change this plan.	_____

MyBookshelf > My eLab > Exercises
> Unit 9 > Strategies

© ERPI • Reproduction prohibited

■ Improve Your Pronunciation: Reduced Speech

A. Say this sentence: I should have applied for the job. I would have been good at it.

Did you pronounce every word clearly and distinctly? In fluent speech, English speakers often do not pronounce every word. *I should have* becomes *I should've*, and *I would have* becomes *I would've*. This is called reduced speech.

Some other common examples are as follows:

Phrases with *and*:   salt and pepper ⟶ salt'n'pepper

                         paper and pen ⟶ paper'n'pen

                         cup and saucer ⟶ cup'n'saucer

Phrases with *to*:   I'm going to ⟶ I'm gonna

                         I want to ⟶ I wanna

                         I have to ⟶ I hafta

Phrases with *or*:   black or white ⟶ black'r'white

                         lunch or dinner ⟶ lunch'r'dinner

                         left or right ⟶ left'r'right

Phrases with *have*:   I might have ⟶ I might've

                         I could have ⟶ I could've

Practise saying these with a partner.

Note: Many instances of reduced speech should never be used in written form. In addition, some instances (*gonna*, *wanna*, *hafta*) should not be used in a formal or academic setting.

B. Listen to the sentences, spoken using reduced speech. Repeat each one.

1. Put some salt and pepper on the table.

2. I don't want to go to work today.

3. Shall we meet one day for lunch or dinner?

4. I'm going to apply for the promotion.

5. I could have been a star if I'd kept dancing.

6. I have to finish my work before I go home.

7. Do you like the logo in red or blue?

8. If I'd known the company was expanding, I wouldn't have quit.

MyBookshelf > My eLab > Exercises
> Unit 9 > Pronunciation

© **ERPI** • Reproduction prohibited

Bring It All Together

A. Read the following memo from company president Franklin Fitzgerald to the human resources department at Fitzgerald Furniture.

As you know, Fitzgerald Furniture has experienced a difficult few months. In this economic downturn, our profits are down, there is a salary freeze in effect, and there will be no end-of-year bonuses this year.

As a result, there is a high level of stress among our workers. Many are worried about losing their jobs, and we appreciate their concerns. However, we are optimistic that the situation will improve and no one will be laid off. Until the situation gets better, we need to find ways to reduce stress among our workforce. We want our employees to be enthusiastic about coming to work. We want them to be motivated to help get this company back on its feet.

I would like you to explore ways in which we can help our workers to deal with stress. We cannot raise salaries, and we cannot offer perks such as trips or cars. We are, however, willing to provide $5,000 to implement your ideas. Remember that we have a workforce of sixty-nine people, equally divided between males and females and ranging in age from nineteen to sixty-four.

We invite you to propose your ideas in the form of a poster, which will be presented to the employees at a staff meeting. Posters will be presented in the Human Resources Office on

B. Work in groups of three. Imagine you are the human resources department for Fitzgerald Furniture. Come up with some strategies to reduce stress among the company's employees. Here are some ideas you could consider:

- Improvements to the workplace, for example, a new paint colour or a garden.
- A day away from the workplace, for example, to the beach or the lake.
- A trip to a spa, a massage therapist, or similar treatment.
- Tickets to a sporting event or musical performance.
- A dinner or party, either at the workplace or elsewhere.
- A company volunteer project, for example, serving dinner at a homeless shelter.

C. Display your ideas on a poster on a separate page. Your teacher will give you poster card, pens, glue, and other supplies. As you design your poster, keep in mind the strategies you have learned in this unit.

D. Share your ideas with your class in the form of a short presentation. Follow these steps:

1. Each group should attach their completed poster to the wall of the classroom. Be sure to allow plenty of space between posters.

2. Each group should elect a spokesperson. That person will stay next to the poster. Other group members should circulate around the room and visit other posters.

3. Spokespeople will explain their group's ideas to anyone who comes by. If possible, invite visitors from other classes. Engage in a discussion with each visitor and share ideas.

4. When your teacher tells you, change the spokesperson. Each group member should have a chance to present the poster.

© ERPI • Reproduction prohibited

E. As a class, take a vote on which group has the best plan. Discuss with your class which ideas you would choose if you worked for Fitzgerald Furniture.

HOW DID YOU DO?

Did your group apply the strategies you have learned in this unit? Fill in the chart below to evaluate your own performance in this activity.

Strategy	Did we do this?		
	Yes	I'm not sure ...	No
We all played positive, supportive roles in the group.			
We created a clear, effective poster.			
Our poster had a mixture of text and pictures or graphs.			
The writing on our poster was easy to read, with a large enough font size and bullet points.			
The design of our poster was logical, not confusing.			
All members made an equal contribution to the activity.			

Go Further

This is a dining and relaxing area for employees at Google's headquarters in Mountain View, California.

A. Work in groups of three or four to discuss the following terms and how they could relate to the workplace. Write a short definition next to each one. You may need to research these terms on the Internet.

1. flex hours: _____

_____

2. bean bag chairs: _____

_____

3. valet parking: _____

_____

© ERPI • Reproduction prohibited

4. open-plan office: _____

_____

5. full kitchen: _____

_____

6. on-site daycare: _____

_____

B. In your groups, discuss the following questions.

1. All of the above are examples of features of some modern workplaces. Which of these do you think would have the most positive impact on a workplace, and why?

2. From your own knowledge and experience, or also from surveying the Internet, what are some other workplace features that could create a very positive workplace environment?

3. If you were an employer, how do you think you would encourage a positive feeling in the workplace?

© **ERPI** • Reproduction prohibited

In this unit, you will learn to do the following:

Think critically about issues related to crime.

Use vocabulary related to feelings about the legal system.

Learn to take part in whole-class discussions.

Discuss a controversial topic with your class.

Understand the use of the /ə/ sound.

IT'S THE LAW

Discuss the Topic

A. Work in pairs. Read the following true stories. With your partner, decide what punishment each person should receive. Choose from the following:

a jail sentence (How long?) | a fine (How much?) | no punishment | another punishment of your choice

Case 1

Welshmen Rhys Jones, twenty-one, and Keri Mules, twenty, were on a working vacation in Australia when they attended a party on the beach. After consuming alcohol, they broke into SeaWorld, swam with the dolphins, and stole a penguin named Dirk. They woke up the following morning to find Dirk in their apartment. They tried to release him into a canal, but witnesses called the police. The pair were arrested, and Dirk was safely returned to his lifelong partner, Peaches.

Our punishment: _____

Case 2

Neil McArdle, thirty-six, from Liverpool, England, forgot to complete all the paperwork required for his wedding. On the day of the wedding, he could not bring himself to confess his mistake to his bride. He made an anonymous phone call to the wedding venue and said there was a bomb in the building. Everyone left the building in a state of panic, and the police were called. They established that phone calls related to the bomb had come from Neil's mobile phone.

Our punishment: _____

Case 3

Anita Krajnc, fifty, an animal rights activist from Toronto, Canada, came across a truck carrying 190 pigs on a hot day. The pigs were on their way to a slaughterhouse. Feeling sympathy for the pigs, Anita gave some of them water from a bottle. The driver of the truck asked her to stop. When she didn't, he called the police. Anita's supporters said she was helping animals that were suffering. Opponents argued that she could have contaminated meat intended for human consumption.

Our punishment: _____

Case 4

American Joy Cassidy, seventy-four, of Boise, Idaho, visited her local library on ten occasions late at night after the library was closed. She poured various liquids into the book return box, including ketchup, mayonnaise, and maple syrup. Library staff would come to work the next day and find damaged books. Joy was arrested when the police sat in wait for her one night and caught her pouring mayonnaise into the box. She claimed she was acting in revenge because she had been banned from using the library.

Our punishment: _____

© ERPI • Reproduction prohibited

B. Which was the most difficult case to agree on? Why? Discuss this question with your class. (See page 134 for the actual punishments.)

Develop Your Vocabulary

A. Work in pairs. Choose the best word or phrase to complete each of the following sentences.

witness | arrest | sentence | probation | felony
community service | jury | trial | house arrest | find ... guilty

1. The judge gave the criminal a _____ of ten years in jail, the maximum penalty for the crime.

2. A serious crime that often results in jail time is known as a _____.

3. The judge appointed a group of twelve men and women to be the _____ in the case.

4. The thief does not have to go to jail, but he has been placed on _____ for two years. This means that if he commits any other crimes, he will have to come back to court.

5. When a crime has been committed, but it is not serious or no one was injured, the criminal may often be told to perform a number of hours of _____.

6. The suspect in the case of the missing bicycle was placed under _____ last night. He is due to appear in court tomorrow.

7. Sometimes a criminal is punished by being told they cannot leave their home except in the case of a health emergency. This is called _____.

8. The police are hoping they can find a _____ to the bank robbery that took place last night.

9. The famous model is on trial for killing her husband. Most people think the jury is going to _____ her _____.

10. So many people wanted to attend the _____ of the accused killer that video cameras were allowed into the courtroom.

© ERPI • Reproduction prohibited

B. Tell your partner about the following:

1. A famous trial you have heard about.

2. Someone you know who was a witness to a crime.

3. A well-known person who was arrested.

4. Whether you would like to be on a jury.

5. The kinds of crimes for which house arrest is a good punishment.

6. The advantages of community service.

MyBookshelf > My eLab > Exercises
> Unit 10 > Vocabulary

Build Your Knowledge

BEFORE YOU WATCH

A. Discuss these questions with your class.

1. Have you heard the English expression "an eye for an eye"? What do you think it means?

2. What do you think is a suitable punishment for these people?

   a) An eighteen-year-old woman who takes a taxi ride, then refuses to pay the driver.

   b) A woman who makes her dog live in a filthy house with no food.

   c) A young man who steals a bicycle.

VIDEO: MEET THE JUDGE WHO WENT VIRAL FOR HIS CREATIVE PUNISHMENTS

B. Watch the video. In this video you will meet judge Michael Cicconetti of Painesville, Ohio. Judge Cicconetti works at the municipal (local) level, dealing with people who have committed minor crimes. He has become famous for giving unusual punishments to the law-breakers who appear in his courtroom.

AFTER YOU WATCH

C. Work in pairs. Answer these questions.

1. **a)** What choice of punishment was Victoria Bascom given for not paying her taxi fare?

   _____ or _____ .

   b) Which did she choose?

   _____

© ERPI • Reproduction prohibited

2. Which punishments were given to these people? Match the criminal with the judge's punishment.

Criminal		Judge's punishment
A man who used the services of a prostitute.		**a)** Be sprayed with pepper spray.
A teenager who stole from an adult bookstore.		**b)** Wear a chicken costume.
A woman who assaulted a fast-food worker.		**c)** Carry a sign saying "See no evil."

3. What percentage of criminals reoffend?

a) Nationally _____

b) In Judge Cicconetti's court _____

4. Why does Judge Cicconetti think it is important to deal with criminals successfully at the municipal level?

_____

_____

_____

5. Case Study: Alyssa Morrow

a) What crime does Alyssa plead guilty to?

_____

b) What choice of punishment does Judge Cicconetti give her?

_____ or _____.

c) What does Alyssa think about her creative punishment?

_____

6. Case Study: Jordan Walsh

a) What crime does Jordan plead guilty to?

_____

b) What choice of punishment does Judge Cicconetti give him?

_____ or _____.

c) What does Jordan think about his creative punishment?

_____

© ERPI • Reproduction prohibited

MyBookshelf > My eLab > Exercises
> Unit 10 > Meet the Judge

Share Your Ideas

≥ Discuss these questions with your whole class.

1. In what way is Judge Cicconetti following the old saying, "an eye for an eye"?

2. What are some advantages of Judge Cicconetti's creative punishments? Use the video and your own ideas to complete the table. The first is done for you. Then, rank these advantages from most important (1) to least important (5).

Advantage	Ranking
It's cheaper to give this kind of punishment than to send someone to jail.	

3. What arguments might opponents of Judge Cicconetti have?

4. Look again at the four true stories in Discuss the Topic (page 124). If these people had appeared in Judge Cicconetti's courtroom, what punishment do you think he might have given each of them?
   a) Rhys Jones and Keri Mules
   b) Neil McArdle
   c) Anita Krajnc
   d) Joy Cassidy

5. "We need more judges like Judge Cicconetti." Do you agree? Why, or why not?

Develop Speaking Fluency: Whole-Class Speaking Activities 1
Address Concerns about Speaking in Front of the Class

If you are planning to study at university or college in an English-speaking country, you will need to take part in whole-class discussions with up to twenty students. These discussions may be called "seminars" or "tutorials." They are a good way to discuss the material you have read about in your textbooks, or that you have heard about in lectures.

Many students are nervous about speaking in front of the entire class. They worry about their English skills, or they think they don't have anything useful to contribute to the discussion. This is always a mistake. Whole-class discussions are a great way to share ideas with a larger group of people and to develop your own thoughts on a topic.

© ERPI • Reproduction prohibited

In college and university classrooms, the professor or instructor will not usually ask specific students to answer questions. Students are expected to decide for themselves whether or not to contribute. It is important that you do so. In many cases, your final grade will include marks for participation in discussions.

Remember that you will be rewarded for expressing your own thoughts and ideas. There is often no "right" or "wrong" answer.

CONCERNS ABOUT SPEAKING IN FRONT OF THE CLASS

Work in pairs. Look at the students' concerns below and decide what suggestions you would give to each one.

1. Elisa doesn't mind speaking in small groups, but she is terrified to speak in front of the entire class. She is afraid no one will understand her.

   _____

   _____

   _____

2. Luis has plenty of good ideas, but he cannot find a way to make himself heard. Every time he tries to enter the conversation, someone louder speaks up, and his voice is lost.

   _____

   _____

   _____

3. Corinna tries very hard to follow class discussions, but she often has difficulty understanding what the other students are saying. Everyone speaks so quickly!

   _____

   _____

   _____

4. Hugo is frustrated because he is often the only person in his class who is prepared for his seminars. The other students don't do the readings, and they have nothing to say in class.

   _____

   _____

   _____

© ERPI • Reproduction prohibited

STRATEGIES FOR DEALING WITH CONCERNS ABOUT SPEAKING IN FRONT OF THE CLASS

You are nervous about speaking in front of the entire class.

Keep these tips in mind:

- Understand that you are not alone. Many students, including native English speakers, are nervous about speaking in front of a large group.

- Make sure you are well prepared for your class. Do your readings and make a note of things you would like to discuss and questions you would like to ask. If you are well prepared, you should have something interesting to say. No one will notice if you use the wrong verb tense or preposition—and if they *do* notice, they won't care.

- Don't delay making a contribution to the discussion. Try to speak up early in the discussion. Once you have spoken in class, contributing will become easier.

- Remember that you don't need to say something unique or original. It's fine to just agree with someone else, or to ask a question. This can help you to build confidence.

- Get to know the people in your class. If you think of them as your friends, you will be less nervous about speaking in front of them.

You find it hard to enter the conversation.

These strategies might help you:

- Don't expect everyone to immediately be quiet when you start to talk. It is normal in group discussions to have to fight to be heard. Stand your ground: don't immediately back down when someone speaks at the same time as you. Try not to pause or hesitate, as this will signal to the class that you have finished.

- Sit in a prominent place in the classroom. If you sit at the back or on the edge of the group, you might be sending a message that you are not interested or involved. Sit in the middle and/or at the front, and your classmates will pay more attention to you.

- Use body language to show that you are involved. Lean forward, look at the person speaking, and show enthusiasm. Someone might notice that you're trying to get into the conversation, and he or she might ask you directly for your opinion.

You have difficulty understanding the discussion.

Try these suggestions:

- Meet a friend or two to discuss the topic of the discussion before the actual class. You could compare notes from your lectures and readings, or you could identify some key areas that you think will come up in the discussion.

- As you do these things, try to develop your listening skills by exposing yourself to as much English as you can. Go to lectures and other events, watch videos, talk to native speakers, and listen to conversations around your campus.

© **ERPI** • Reproduction prohibited

You are the only person who is willing to talk.

These tips should be helpful:

- See your situation as an opportunity to get to know the instructor. You will have some great discussions, and you should get excellent participation marks.

- See yourself as a class leader. One of the best ways to really learn new material is to teach it. Don't be afraid to offer explanations to less-confident students.

Whatever your concern ...

In all cases, don't be afraid to speak to your instructor or seminar leader to share your concerns. They understand that not everyone learns in the same way, and that some people are naturally quieter than others. They will realize that you are a serious student, and they will try to help you with your concerns.

MyBookshelf > My eLab > Exercises
> Unit 10 > Strategies

Improve Your Pronunciation: Unstressed Syllables—Using /ə/

A. Say this sentence: The library books were covered with ketchup, mayonnaise, and syrup.

Several of the words in this sentence have more than one syllable: *library*, *covered*, *ketchup*, *mayonnaise*, and *syrup*. In English, not every syllable is given equal stress. When a syllable is not stressed, the vowel sound it contains is often changed into an /ə/ sound. The /ə/ sound is pronounced /uh/.

The /ə/ sound is the most common sound in English. Knowing when to use an /ə/ sound can make your pronunciation much more natural.

B. Look again at these words. With a partner, decide whether each syllable is stressed or unstressed. Underline the unstressed vowel sound(s) in each word. Practise saying the words.

  1. library

  2. covered

  3. ketchup

  4. mayonnaise

  5. syrup

© ERPI • Reproduction prohibited

C. With a partner, look at these sentences. Underline each vowel that you would pronounce with an /ə/ sound. (Hint: don't focus on spelling; the /ə/ sound can replace any vowel sound.)

1. Call the police! Someone's taken the penguin.

2. He's a young offender, so he won't go to prison.

3. Two brothers were arrested for the murder of their parents.

4. Do you agree with the saying, "an eye for an eye"?

5. The criminal was given a suspended sentence.

6. Arson is considered a serious crime in Canada.

7. My car has been stolen. I need to find a witness.

8. The man from England was placed under house arrest.

D. Listen to the sentences. Repeat each one.

MyBookshelf > My eLab > Exercises
> Unit 10 > Pronunciation

Bring It All Together

A. Read the following update from Northbright College.

Three students involved in last year's protest at the office of George Penner, Vice-President of Student Services, have been found guilty of trespassing and destruction of property. Jack Pierce, nineteen, Suzy Lee, twenty, and Jamal Jones, twenty-four, will be sentenced next month. The prosecutor in the case has recommended each student be fined $5,000 and serve a thirty-day jail term. The lawyer for the defendants has asked for probation.

The three were identified as the leaders of a group of about twenty-five students who went to Penner's office at about nine a.m. on January 23rd of last year to protest various decisions, including cutting funding for food services and increasing the cost of bus passes. The students say they were protesting peacefully, but administrative support workers left because they felt they were in danger. Penner's senior administrative assistant, Alice Bone, sixty-one, fell and hurt her foot on the way out; she claimed she had been pushed by one of the protesters. Penner himself was not injured. He tried to discuss the matter with the students, but he left the office at around seven p.m. He has not returned to work, and is currently undergoing medical treatment for stress.

The group refused to leave Penner's office for five days. At first, there was a "fun" atmosphere, as students in the group played music and gave live interviews to the local radio station. Other students held parties outside and carried signs supporting the protesters. Soon, however, the protest turned aggressive and there was damage to the administrative building. Some furniture was damaged, and windows were broken.

The college gave a deadline of nine p.m. on January 28th for the students to leave without facing any charges. Most of the twenty-five students did leave. The university then turned off power and water to the administrative building, and eventually, the remaining three protesters left. They were arrested and charged with trespassing and destruction of property. The judge in the case, Aaron Cunningham, is willing to listen to recommendations regarding sentencing from the Northbright community. Northbright is also considering expelling the three students.

© **ERPI** • Reproduction prohibited

B. You are going to take part in a class discussion. Each member of the class will play the role of someone connected to the demonstration. See page 160 for a list of the roles. Some of you will be supportive of the three students and think they should receive a light punishment, or no punishment at all. Some of you will demand a stronger punishment. Follow these steps:

1. Your teacher will give you a piece of paper with your role number. Turn to page 160 where you will find details about a person who is connected to the protest. Your character is attending an open meeting at the university to discuss the university's position on the sentencing of Pierce, Lee, and Jones.

2. Read about your character. Don't share your role identity with anyone else.

3. Take five minutes and make notes about your argument on a separate page. How will you argue that your opinion is best?

4. Your teacher will lead an open meeting in which various members of the Northbright community are welcome to express their opinions on the case and to make recommendations regarding sentencing. Anyone is welcome to express any opinion at any time. Based on the discussion, a recommendation will be made to Judge Cunningham.

C. As a class, take a vote on which form of punishment would be most suitable for the three students.

HOW DID YOU DO?

Did you apply the strategies you have learned in this unit? Fill in the chart below to evaluate your own performance in this activity.

	Did I do this?		
Strategy	**Yes**	**I'm not sure ...**	**No**
I entered the discussion within the first few minutes.			
I played an active role in the discussion.			
I didn't let other people interrupt me.			
I was able to express my opinions.			
I used body language to show my willingness to talk.			

Go Further

This is Christopher Thomas Knight, also known as the "North Pond Hermit." He lived in the forest in rural Maine, USA, for twenty-seven years, with no known human contact.

A. Work in groups of three or four. Use the Internet to answer the following questions.

1. How did Christopher Thomas Knight survive in the woods for so many years?

_____

_____

2. What crimes did he commit in order to survive?

_____

_____

3. What did people think about him? Find several different opinions.

_____

_____

_____

4. How was he finally caught?

_____

_____

5. What was his punishment from the legal system?

_____

_____

B. In your groups, discuss the following questions.

1. Do you think Christopher Thomas Knight should have been sent to jail?

2. What kind of punishment do you think Judge Cicconetti would have given him?

3. How could Knight make a contribution to society after his jail sentence?

The actual punishments from Discuss the Topic (page 124):
1. Rhys Jones and Keri Mules were each fined $1,000 and ordered to write a letter of apology to SeaWorld.
2. Neil McArdle was sentenced to a year in prison.
3. Anita Krajnc received no punishment. The judge said no crime had been committed.
4. Joy Cassidy was sentenced to a month in jail and had to pay over $3,000 to replace the books.

© **ERPI** • Reproduction prohibited

In this unit, you will learn to do the following:

Think critically about issues related to playing games online.

Use vocabulary related to playing games online.

Develop strategies for speaking persuasively.

Take part in a debate.

Use appropriate stress for compound nouns.

ONLINE GAMES

Discuss the Topic

A. Work in pairs. Discuss the following questions.

1. Do you ever play online games? Choose one of the following answers:

   ☐ Yes, I love playing online games. I play them regularly.

   ☐ I have played these games, but I no longer play them.

   ☐ No, I have never played one of these games.

2. If you play online, what is the difference between playing with other people and playing a game alone? Which do you prefer?

3. What are the most popular games among your group of friends? What is most appealing about these particular games?

4. If you play online games, how much time do you spend doing so? In your opinion, how much time spent playing online is too much?

5. How can you tell when someone is spending too much time playing online games?

B. What do you think are the dangers of playing online games? Discuss this question with your class.

Develop Your Vocabulary

A. Work in pairs. Match each word with the correct meaning.

Words		Meanings
1. massive (adjective)		**a)** feeling of nervousness and anxiety
2. hand-eye coordination (noun)		**b)** ongoing feeling of deep sadness
3. addiction (noun)		**c)** unable to concentrate on a task
4. tension (noun)		**d)** hands and sight working together
5. motor skills (noun)		**e)** feeling of being tired
6. distracted (adjective)		**f)** movements of the muscles
7. fatigue (noun)		**g)** existing online
8. concentration (noun)		**h)** very large
9. virtual (adjective)		**i)** inability to give up something
10. depression (noun)		**j)** ability to focus on something

© ERPI • Reproduction prohibited

B. Now use each word in a sentence of your own.

1. massive: _____

2. hand-eye coordination: _____

3. addiction: _____

4. tension: _____

5. motor skills: _____

6. distracted: _____

7. fatigue: _____

8. concentration: _____

9. virtual: _____

10. depression: _____

C. Tell your partner about the following:

1. An activity you do that requires hand-eye coordination.

2. A situation that causes tension in your life.

3. Something that causes you to become distracted.

4. What you do when you are experiencing fatigue.

5. Something you do that requires concentration.

6. A piece of advice you would give to someone suffering from depression.

MyBookshelf > My eLab > Exercises
> Unit 11 > Vocabulary

Build Your Knowledge

BEFORE YOU READ

A. Discuss these questions with your class.

1. What do you understand by the term MMORPG?

2. Do you have any experiences with MMORPGs?

3. What do you think are the effects of MMORPGs, both positive and negative?

B. Work in pairs. Read the paragraphs below. Put them in the correct order to create an article about the positive and negative effects of MMORPGs.

_____ There are many studies which show that playing online games regularly has positive effects on players. For example, people who play these games often show good development of motor skills and also hand-eye coordination, since a great deal of physical movement is necessary to pay attention to the action on the screens and react to it. Players can also benefit mentally, as the need for intense concentration is a factor in being successful. Concentration is a skill useful to people in many different situations in their lives. Similarly, with the amount of information to be absorbed in these games, the memory of players can often improve. And, while some people worry about the social skills of those who play games, MMORPGs, with the involvement of millions of players from around the world, can actually help promote relationships, as players form friendships in virtual communities.

_____ The rise in popularity of MMORPGs reflect what is for many a fun hobby, a chance to play games with others from around the world, and to enjoy the new world created online. It's also a great way to improve your physical and mental skills. However, it's important to be aware of the potential dangers of these games. Don't allow the online world to take over the real one.

_____ However, studies have also shown that players who spend a great deal of time playing games may experience forms of addiction, similar to addiction to alcohol, tobacco, and so on. The most obvious symptoms include feelings of tension when not playing and ignoring other people. Players may also notice themselves getting distracted or anxious when not online, and spending all their time thinking about when they can next go online to play. Addicted players may experience fatigue, since it's common to stay up very late playing games. They may also experience headaches, caused by staring at the screen for hours at a time. Players who cannot force themselves to stop playing may also have poor personal hygiene, since they don't want to stop playing to take a shower. Eventually, some of these effects can lead to long-term sleeping and eating disorders and to pain. Mental health can also be negatively affected by game addiction, as addicted players suffer from depression based on events in the online world.

_____ Years ago, video games or computer games were an activity played by one person on his or her own. But now, a single person can be joined by millions of others around the world, in an online gaming environment. These popular games are known as MMORPGs—massive multiplayer online role-playing games. Some of the best known are _World of Warcraft_ and the hugely popular _Fortnite_. Like many popular activities, millions of people have lots of fun playing them, and they can have positive effects on their players. On the other hand, some psychologists are increasingly concerned about possible mental and physical effects of online gaming.

_____ Given these concerns, it is important that players of online games take measures to ensure that their gaming doesn't negatively affect their lives. Players need to play smart and avoid any problems that online gaming addiction can cause. How can you tell whether or not you are playing smart? Pay attention to how much time you spend online; if you need to rush back to your room from class to play, that may be a warning sign that you are too caught up in the game. Are you losing sleep because

© ERPI • Reproduction prohibited

your fellow gamers live in another time zone? Are you missing classes or calling in sick to work? Pay attention, too, to your friends. If you suspect a friend is spending too much time playing games online, don't hesitate to talk to that person. For people who have real problems trying to spend less time online gaming, it may be necessary to seek professional help. This does require a time commitment, but this is far better than spending more time online at the risk of physical and mental health problems. The aim should be to have fun and not get caught up in problems.

AFTER YOU READ

C. Work in pairs. Answer these questions.

1. What are five positive effects of playing MMORPGs?

a) _____

b) _____

c) _____

d) _____

e) _____

2. What are some possible signs of addiction to online games?

a) _____ f) _____

b) _____ g) _____

c) _____ h) _____

d) _____ i) _____

e) _____

3. How can you tell whether you might be spending too much time playing games online?

_____

_____

4. How can a friend help someone else with game addiction?

_____

_____

5. What should game players worried about addiction do for themselves?

_____

_____

© **ERPI** • Reproduction prohibited

D. Use your answers to these questions to summarize the concern about MMORPGs in your own words.

MyBookshelf > My eLab > Exercises
> Unit 11 > The Positive and Negative
Effects of MMORPGs

Share Your Ideas

Discuss these questions with your whole class.

1. Why do you think MMORPGs have become so popular in recent years?

2. In your experience playing games, or in observing your friends, do you see evidence of some of the positive or negative effects of game-playing mentioned in the article? Give some examples.

3. Imagine these MMORPG players are your friends. Would you be concerned about them? Give each one a number as follows:

1 – I'm very worried about this friend.
2 – This friend needs to be careful, but at the moment I'm not worried.
3 – I'm not at all worried about this friend.

Sophie is an expert at *Fortnite*. She says she can beat anyone. She spends around ten hours playing *Fortnite* every week. She also goes to class, has a part-time job, and plays sports.	————
Ben plays *World of Warcraft*. He schedules one hour every day for this activity. He doesn't like to miss his scheduled time; he has even planned his university timetable to accommodate his daily game hour.	————
Alice has started to play *Lord of the Rings*. Because she is studying overseas, she finds herself playing in the middle of the night so she can play with people from her home country.	————
Martin's favourite game is *Star Wars*. He recently missed a party for his parents' wedding anniversary because he was in the middle of a game and completely forgot about it.	————
Kate spent five days last month in her college dorm room playing *Dungeons and Dragons* and eating candy bars. She didn't take a shower. Her parents tried to reach her, and she ignored her phone.	————

4. In 2018, the Vancouver Canucks hockey team banned their players from playing *Fortnite* and other video games while travelling for away games. Why do you think they did this? Do you think the team made the right decision? Explain your answer.

© ERPI • Reproduction prohibited

Develop Speaking Fluency: Whole-Class Speaking Activities 2

Speak Persuasively

There is often no "right" or "wrong" answer in class discussions. However, you will need to think critically about a topic and express your opinions in a way that convinces other people that you are right. This is called persuasive speaking. It is different from persuasive essay writing, since you are using spoken words instead of written words. A good way to develop skills in persuasive speaking is through debating.

A PERSUASIVE SPEAKER

A. Work in groups of three or four. Discuss the following questions.

1. Can you think of anyone famous (past or present) who is known for being a strong public speaker? This should be someone who has the ability to convince other people that his or her opinions are the best. This could be a politician, a business leader, or another public figure. This may be someone known internationally or only in your country.

   Speaker: _____

2. What makes this person a good speaker? What do you notice when this person speaks? If you can, find a video online of this person speaking. Show the video to your group, and share your reactions.

   _____

   _____

   _____

STRATEGIES FOR SPEAKING PERSUASIVELY

B. In your groups, look at the following strategies for speaking persuasively. Decide whether you should or should not do each one. Underline *Do* or *Don't*. Then choose the best reason for your answer.

1. **Do | Don't** research your arguments before you give them because …
   a) This is not a research essay; you don't need to give much detail.
   b) You cannot argue something unless you understand it well.

2. **Do | Don't** use formal, high-level words because …
   a) Your listeners will admire your intelligence, and they will trust your opinions.
   b) Your listeners will think you're putting on an act to impress them.

© ERPI • Reproduction prohibited

3. Do | Don't use long sentences and complex sentence structure because …

    a) You need to keep the language simple so that no one is confused about your message.

    b) You need to show your listeners that you have thought carefully about your opinions.

4. Do | Don't use statistics in your speech because …

    a) These are boring; your listeners will fall asleep.

    b) A few carefully chosen statistics can make your argument stronger.

5. Do | Don't tell stories that cause an emotional response because …

    a) These can make your argument more convincing.

    b) You need to convince your listeners with facts, not with emotions.

6. Do | Don't speak a little slower when you make your main points because …

    a) This tells your audience that what you are saying is important.

    b) Your audience might get bored and stop paying attention.

7. Do | Don't pause while you are giving your argument because …

    a) You don't have time; you have too much to say.

    b) Your listeners need time to process what you're saying.

WHAT ABOUT BODY LANGUAGE?

C. Your body language is just as important as your speaking style. With your group, write a check mark ✓ next to the things you should do. Write an ✗ next to things you should not do.

☐ Make eye contact with your listeners.

☐ Use hand gestures to emphasize your most important points.

☐ Put your hands in your pockets.

☐ If you are sitting down, lean forward in your chair.

☐ If you are standing, stand up straight.

☐ Look at the teacher while you're talking.

☐ Walk around the room as much as possible.

☐ Smile.

D. Go back to the video you found in task A. Which of the body language tips does your chosen speaker do? In what ways is the speaker's body language effective? Discuss with your group.

MyBookshelf > My eLab > Exercises
> Unit 11 > Strategies

© **ERPI** • Reproduction prohibited

■ Improve Your Pronunciation: Compound Nouns

A. Say this sentence: Playing this computer game has really improved my motor skills.

The phrase *computer game* is a *compound noun*. A compound noun is formed when two words are interpreted as a single unit. *Motor skills* is another example of a compound noun.

Compound nouns can be *open*—made up of two separate words. Examples are *eye contact, social skills*, or *delete key*.

Compound nouns can also be closed—made into a single word. Examples are *website, database,* and *backspace.*

Don't confuse compound nouns with simple adjective + noun combinations. For example:

• The US President lives in the *White House*. This is treated as a single unit.

• I live in a *white house*. This is a simple adjective + noun grouping.

When you see a compound noun, it is important to remember that the stress always comes on the first part.

B. With a partner, look at these compound nouns. Try saying each one, with the stress on the first word.

1. game addiction
2. role-play
3. home page
4. touchscreen

5. screensaver
6. space bar
7. voicemail
8. text message

9. laser printer
10. power cord
11. webcam
12. keyboard

C. Now listen to the following sentences. Repeat each one.

1. Poor hygiene can be a sign of game addiction.
2. Do you enjoy doing role-play activities in class?
3. If classes are cancelled, you will see a message on the college's home page.
4. I have never enjoyed using a touchscreen computer.
5. My favourite screensaver is my collection of vacation pictures.
6. Sarah developed thumb pain from hitting the space bar so often.
7. I left a voicemail for the chair of the department.
8. Johnny was too busy to call his girlfriend so he sent her a text message.
9. Adam is really pleased with his new laser printer.
10. Maggie left her power cord in the library.
11. Cover your webcam with a piece of tape so no one can spy on you.
12. My keyboard has both English and French characters.

© **ERPI** • Reproduction prohibited

D. Work in groups of three or four. How many other compound nouns can you think of that are not related to computers? Complete the chart.

basketball				
dining room				

MyBookshelf > My eLab > Exercises
> Unit 11 > Pronunciation

Bring It All Together

You are going to take part in a debate. In the debate, you will work in pairs to formulate and present an argument in favour of, or against, a point of view. You will debate your topic, called the *motion*, in front of the class.

Each debate will have two students who are in favour of the motion and two who are against it. Your teacher (or a student who is not debating the topic) will act as moderator, with responsibility for making sure the debate process is followed correctly. The pair in favour of the motion will sit at the front of the class, on the moderator's right-hand side. The pair against the motion will sit on the moderator's left-hand side.

During the debate, the speakers must listen politely to each other and not interrupt. Likewise, the audience members cannot interrupt. They will have an opportunity to ask questions later.

After all speakers have presented their arguments, the members of the audience may ask questions, respond to arguments, and make further points.

The debate ends with a vote on which team has presented the most convincing argument, either in favour of the motion, or against it. The vote could be a show of hands, or it could be a secret vote. Don't vote according to what you personally believe about the motion; vote on the basis of each team's quality of presentation and powers of persuasion.

The structure of the debate is as follows.

Stage	Language You Can Use
1. Moderator: Introduction to the debate and introduction of first speaker	• Ladies and gentlemen, today we are debating the motion "[insert motion]." Speaking in favour of the motion we have [name] and [name]. Speaking against the motion are [name] and [name]. The rules are as follows. [Moderator should outline the rules above.] • I now call upon [name] to offer the first arguments in favour of the motion.
2. Team in Favour, Student A Presentation of first arguments 3 minutes	• Thank you. We strongly believe that the motion "[motion]" is correct. • I would like to start with … • The first reason why we agree with the motion is that … • There is no doubt that … • Research has shown that … • Statistics from [source] show that … • Another argument in favour of the motion is that … • It is clear, therefore, that …

© **ERPI** • Reproduction prohibited

Stage	Language You Can Use
3. Moderator: Introduction of second speaker	• Thank you, [name]. Our second speaker is [name], who will argue against the motion.
4. Team Against, Student A Presentation of first arguments 3 minutes	• Thank you. [name] has told us that _____. However, we would like to argue that … • Despite what [name] says, we believe that … • The first reason why we disagree with the motion is that … • There is no doubt that … • Research has shown that … • Statistics from [source] show that … • Another argument against the motion is that … • It is clear, therefore, that …
5. Moderator: Introduction of third speaker	• Thank you, [name]. Our third speaker is [name], who will offer further points in favour of the motion.
6. Team in Favour, Student B Presentation of second arguments 3 minutes	• Thank you. My partner [name] has told us that _____. There are some other reasons why we believe that … • There is no doubt that … • Research has shown that … • Statistics from [source] show that … • To summarize our main points … • For all of the reasons given by [name] and myself, it is clear that the motion "[insert motion]" must stand.
7. Moderator: Introduction of fourth speaker	• Thank you, [name]. Our final speaker is [name], who will offer further points against the motion.
8. Team Against, Student B Presentation of second arguments 3 minutes	• Thank you. My partner [name] has told us that _____. There are some other reasons why we believe that … • There is no doubt that … • Research has shown that … • Statistics from [source] show that … • To summarize our main points … • For all of the reasons given by [name] and myself, it is clear that the motion "[insert motion]" must be defeated.
9. Moderator: Questions from the audience	• Thank you to all of our speakers. I would now like to open the floor to any questions from audience members.
10. Moderator: Vote	• If no one has any further questions, we can take a vote on who has given the most convincing arguments. • I would like to declare that the winner of the debate is the team of [name] and [name]. Therefore, the motion "[insert motion]" stands / is defeated.

© **ERPI** • Reproduction prohibited

A. Work in groups of four. Decide on your debate topic.

With your teacher, each group chooses one of the motions from the list below.

- Playing online games is a good way to learn a second language.
- Games like *Fortnite* and *World of Warcraft* encourage people to be violent.
- Online role-playing games should be banned in high schools.
- Online games are good for children's cognitive development.

Two of you will support the motion, and the other two will oppose it. You don't need to personally hold the beliefs that you are arguing. The goal is to develop skills in speaking in a persuasive manner.

B. Research and plan your arguments.

Each pair (supporters and opposition) researches the topic. You can do this in class or at home. On a separate page, make notes on the arguments you want to make, and on the details you will use to support your argument.

Decide who will talk about each of the points. Each speaker will speak for three minutes.

As you are planning what to say, you should also think about what the opposing team might argue. You should be prepared to speak against the arguments they put forward. Don't let the opposing team members see your notes.

C. Carry out the debate.

Each group of four will debate their chosen motion in front of the class. Follow the process and suggested language shown above.

HOW DID YOU DO?

Did your team apply the strategies you have learned in this unit? Fill in the chart below to evaluate your own performance in this activity.

Strategy	Did we do this?		
	Yes	I'm not sure ...	No
We researched the topic and established our opinions.			
We planned our debate strategy.			
We supported our main points with factual details.			
We spoke in simple, clear language.			
We paid attention to our body language.			
We made a convincing argument.			

© **ERPI** • Reproduction prohibited

Go Further

These people are taking part in an international online gaming tournament.

A. Work in groups of three or four. Use the Internet to answer the following questions.

1. What is meant by the term "eSports?"

_____

_____

2. What are some of the most popular games played?

_____

_____

3. What prizes are available to the winners?

_____

_____

4. If you want to take part in an online tournament, what should you do?

_____

_____

5. It is possible to be a professional player of online games. True or false?

_____

_____

B. In your groups, discuss the following questions.

1. Do you think eSports will one day be accepted by sporting organizations such as the Olympics? Why, or why not?

2. Do you think it is interesting to watch people taking part in eSports? Why, or why not?

3. If your friend told you he or she wanted to become a professional online gamer, what would you say to him or her?

In this unit, you will learn to do the following:

Think critically about issues related to movies.

Use vocabulary related to aspects of movies.

Practise taking part in whole-class discussions.

Lead a discussion with your class.

Address individual pronunciation challenges.

Review the strategies you have developed through this book.

ON THE SCREEN

Discuss the Topic

A. Choose a movie that you have seen recently. Fill in the box with your own answers to the questions below. Then, work in groups of four. Take notes on your classmates' movies.

1. What is the name of the movie?
2. What is the genre of the movie?
3. What is the setting of the movie?
4. Who are the main characters?

5. What is the plot?
6. How did the movie end?
7. How did the movie make you feel?
8. Would you recommend this movie?

Your name:

Student:

Student:

Student:

B. Based on your discussion, is there a movie that you now want to see? Share your thoughts with your class.

© ERPI • Reproduction prohibited

Develop Your Vocabulary

A. Work in pairs. Choose the correct word to complete each sentence. Use a dictionary to help you, if necessary.

1. What is your favourite movie _____? Do you like action movies, or thrillers, or romantic comedies?

   a) genre

   b) plot

2. The *Harry Potter* film _____ had eight movies, one more than the books.

   a) series

   b) sequel

3. Every *James Bond* movie has a similar _____: the hero tries to stop the schemes of an evil villain.

   a) character

   b) plot

4. Spiderman can be considered a good _____ for young viewers; children learn that those who have power should also have responsibility.

   a) stereotype

   b) role model

5. The _____ of *The Sound of Music* was Salzburg, Austria, before World War II.

   a) setting

   b) genre

6. Some people complain that film versions of classic fairy tales include _____s of people from certain countries.

   a) plot

   b) stereotype

7. *Titanic* is based on a real event, but the _____s of Jack and Rose are fictional.

   a) role model

   b) character

8. The first *Mamma Mia* movie was filmed on location in Greece to give it an _____ setting.

   a) authentic

   b) series

9. *Crazy Rich Asians* is one of a small number of Hollywood _____s with an Asian cast.

   a) blockbuster

   b) sequel

10. *The Godfather Part II* was the first _____ to win an Academy Award for Best Picture.

    a) setting

    b) sequel

© **ERPI** • Reproduction prohibited

B. Tell your partner about the following:

1. A blockbuster movie that you personally thought was terrible.

2. A movie plot that you thought was too complex or not realistic.

3. A movie that you think provides a good role model for children.

4. A character that reminded you of yourself, or of someone you know.

5. A movie that you wish had a sequel.

6. A movie with a character that you thought was a stereotype.

MyBookshelf > My eLab > Exercises
> Unit 12 > Vocabulary

Build Your Knowledge

BEFORE YOU WATCH

A. Discuss these questions with your class.

1. Have you seen the movie *Black Panther*? If so, explain the movie to your classmates who have not seen it.

2. In what ways is this movie different from other superhero movies?

VIDEO: XHOSA AND THE *BLACK PANTHER* MOVIE

B. Watch the video. In this video, you will learn about an African language heard in the movie *Black Panther*. See if you can pronounce the name of the language!

AFTER YOU WATCH

C. Work in pairs. Answer these questions.

1. What do you learn from the video about the Xhosa language?

_____

_____

2. Why, according to *Black Panther* actress Danai Gurira, was it important to include Xhosa in the movie?

_____

_____

© **ERPI** • Reproduction prohibited

3. Who was the world's most famous speaker of Xhosa?

_____

4. In what way does Zolani Mahola think the movie gives audiences a new experience?

_____

_____

MyBookshelf > My eLab > Exercises
> Unit 12 > XHOSA and the _Black Panther_ Movie

Share Your Ideas

⚡ **Discuss these questions with your whole class.**

1. _Black Panther_ is one of the most successful movies of all time. In its opening weekend, the movie made more than $150 million. Why do you think it has been so successful? Has it been successful because of the plot, the characters, the use of African themes, or something else?

2. In showing black actors speaking Xhosa, as well as costumes based on African tribal clothing, _Black Panther_ has been described as "not colour blind, but colour brave." What do you think this means?

3. _Black Panther_ actress Lupita Nyong'o grew up in Kenya. She has spoken about the importance of movies like _Black Panther_ for young black children. In what ways can _Black Panther_ be helpful to these children?

4. Can you think of any blockbuster movies that portray people from your own culture? How are they portrayed? Do you think this is accurate?

5. Is there a movie industry in your home country? What kinds of films are produced? What are the main genres, plots, and characters? Do you think your country's film industry produces high-quality films, or could it be improved? Why?

© **ERPI** • Reproduction prohibited

Develop Speaking Fluency: Whole-Class Speaking Activities 3

Lead a Group Discussion

At times during your studies, or in your workplace, you may be asked to lead a discussion on a particular topic. If you are leading a discussion, you have two main goals:

a) to ensure that all participants understand the topic you are discussing; in a college or university setting, this often takes the form of a class presentation; and

b) to encourage members of the group to express their thoughts on the topic, perhaps with the goal of reaching a consensus.

In many cases, your discussion will start with a presentation, in which you provide an overview of the main issue(s). This may be a quick summary, or it may be a formal presentation. If you are asked to give a formal presentation, refer to Units 5 and 6 in this book for strategies for planning and giving your talk.

STRATEGIES FOR LEADING A DISCUSSION

> Work in pairs. Decide which strategies are useful when leading a group discussion. Then discuss your ideas with your class. There may be no "correct" answer.

Strategy	Do	Don't	It depends
1. Make it clear from the beginning what your discussion is about.			
2. Prepare your questions before the discussion, so you know what to cover.			
3. Prepare a handout so class members can follow the main points of the discussion.			
4. Stand up so you are seen as an authority figure and people listen to you.			
5. Do most of the talking. You are the leader, and your job is to teach the others.			
6. Introduce a mixture of general questions and more specific topics for discussion.			
7. Use open-ended questions, e.g. "Why do you think …?" rather than "Do you agree?"			
8. Allow the discussion to go in a different direction from what you had planned.			

© ERPI • Reproduction prohibited

Strategy	Do	Don't	It depends
9. Identify people who have not said anything, and address questions to them.			
10. Review the main ideas at the end.			

MyBookshelf > My eLab > Exercises
> Unit 12 > Strategies

Improve Your Pronunciation

In this final unit, you are going to focus on an aspect of English pronunciation that causes difficulties for you. This may be something that has been covered in this book, or it may be something else entirely.

A. Working alone, identify an aspect of English pronunciation that you find difficult. Write it here:

_____

From this point, you may want to work with a partner who has identified the same aspect of pronunciation as you.

B. Write seven words or sentences that contain this pronunciation challenge.

a) _____

b) _____

c) _____

d) _____

e) _____

f) _____

g) _____

C. Why do you think this particular aspect of pronunciation is challenging? Your answer may be one or more of these:

a) The sound doesn't exist in your first language.

b) You cannot hear the difference between this sound and another.

c) You are not sure what your mouth should be doing.

d) Other reasons that you can relate to.

Write your reason(s) here: _____

_____

© ERPI • Reproduction prohibited

D. What might be some ways of addressing this pronunciation challenge? Write your ideas here:

_____

_____

E. You are now going to lead a short discussion about this aspect of pronunciation to your class. You will have ten minutes. Do the following:

a) Explain what the difficulty is.

b) Give some examples of words or sentences that contain this pronunciation challenge.

c) Say why you think this aspect of pronunciation is difficult.

d) Give advice on how to improve this aspect of pronunciation.

e) Find out about your classmates' experiences with this aspect of communication, and gather any useful tips they may have.

MyBookshelf > My eLab > Exercises
> Unit 12 > Pronunciation

Bring It All Together

With your class, discuss the questions below. You may discuss these in any order you choose. As you take part in these discussions, keep in mind the strategies you have practised for:

- Speaking with confidence.

- Giving opinions.

- Asking others for their opinions.

- Responding to opinions.

- Dealing with problems in discussions.

© ERPI • Reproduction prohibited

1. One of the most popular movie series of recent years has been *The Hunger Games*. The plot of these movies is about teenagers who take part in a fight to the death. How do you explain the popularity of these movies?

2. Many film series have an increasing number of sequels. Can you think of a series where you think too many sequels have been made? Why?

3. Some people have read all of the *Harry Potter* books; some people have only seen the movies. What are the advantages of watching a movie over reading a book? Which do you prefer?

4. Can you think of a popular film that has a strong lesson about society? Give an example of something you have learned or thought about from watching a movie.

5. Can you think of a movie in which characters from one culture are played by actors of another culture? Do you think this is a problem? Why, or why not?

6. One of the most popular films of all time is *Titanic*. Is it important for historical films to be accurate, or is the entertainment value more important? Have you ever learned about history from a movie?

7. Many of today's most popular movies are about superheroes with special powers. Do you wish there were more movies that told stories about ordinary people? Why, or why not?

8. What is a movie that you find yourself often watching again and again? Why do you enjoy this movie so much? What is so compelling about it?

9. One of the longest-running movie series of all time is the *James Bond* series, which began in 1964. How do you explain its ongoing popularity after more than fifty years?

10. Do you ever watch old, classic movies like *Gone with the Wind* or *Casablanca*? If so, why do you like them? If not, why not?

FINAL SELF-EVALUATION

Fill in the chart below with the ten most important strategies you have learned from this book. Do you now use these strategies effectively?

Strategy	Do I do this now?		
	Yes	I'm not sure ...	No
1.			
2.			
3.			
4.			
5.			
6.			
7.			
8.			
9.			
10.			

© **ERPI** • Reproduction prohibited

Go Further

This is Ryan Coogler, director of the blockbuster movie *Black Panther*.

A. Work in groups of three or four. Use the Internet to answer the following questions.

1. How old was Ryan Coogler when he signed a contract to make *Black Panther*?

_____

_____

2. What did he study in college? What else did he do during his studies?

_____

_____

3. How did he get his start in the movie business?

_____

_____

4. What was the subject of his first major film?

_____

_____

5. What significant list was Ryan Coogler on in 2013?

_____

_____

B. In your groups, discuss the following questions.

1. *Black Panther* has been one of the most successful movies in American film history. In what way was it an advantage to have such a young director?

2. Why do you think he was named to *Time*'s list in 2013?

3. If you could ask Ryan any question about his career, what would you ask?

© ERPI • Reproduction prohibited

ANSWERS

Strategies for Leading a Discussion pages 153–154

1. DO. You should always set the parameters for the discussion so the other members of the group know what will and will not be covered.

2. DO. This is a good idea as it will help you to stay focused. If you are nervous and your mind goes blank, you will have a list of subject areas to remind you.

3. IT DEPENDS. It's always a nice idea to introduce a visual aid, but in some informal discussions it may not be necessary, especially if you are using slides.

4. IT DEPENDS. If your discussion follows a slide presentation, you are likely to be already standing. Otherwise, it may be preferable to sit down.

5. DON'T. Your goal is to encourage a discussion, not to lecture to your group.

6. DO. A mix of questions will get everyone talking.

7. DO. Closed questions (i.e., those that can be answered with "yes" or "no") tend not to go anywhere. Open-ended questions lead to a better exchange of ideas.

8. IT DEPENDS. Usually, it is better to stay with the plan you made before the discussion. However, there may be cases where a digression to another topic provokes a useful and interesting discussion. If you feel yourself losing control of the discussion, don't be afraid to bring it back to the original plan.

9. IT DEPENDS. Don't embarrass quiet students by singling them out. However, if you can tell that someone is trying to enter the conversation and is being drowned out, by all means address a point specifically to that person.

10. DO. It is nice to finish the discussion with a summary of the main points that were raised.

© ERPI • Reproduction prohibited

APPENDIX

Bring It All Together, page 20

Sam's Baseball Team

Sam is seventeen and is on his school's baseball team. He is a weaker player and is not given many opportunities to play. Sam argues that they are not professionals; they are high-school students who want to have fun. He says staying healthy is more important than winning games. Should the coach give more playing time to the stronger players, or should all players at the high-school level be given an equal chance?

Ben's Night Out

The Wolves are travelling for an ice hockey tournament. Before they left, the coach told the players that anyone who behaved badly while they were away would be sent home. Ben was caught staying out and dancing in a nightclub. However, he is the team's leading goal scorer, and the team really needs him. Should the coach send him home?

Johanna's Big Decision

The top three members of a gymnastics club can go to a national competition. At a local tournament, the top three in the fourteen to eighteen age group were Caroline, Traci, and Johanna. Kelly is the star of the club, but she was sick on the day of the tournament and came fourth. Should Johanna, who came third, give up her place? Both girls really want to go to the national competition. The coach says it is Johanna's decision.

Quinn's Choice

Quinn plays on his university basketball team. His team has reached the final, but the game is at the same time as his older brother's graduation from medical school. Quinn's brother has told him that he doesn't need to attend, and that he should play in the basketball game. However, his parents want him to go to the graduation. Should Quinn miss the final and go to his brother's graduation? Or should he be loyal to his team?

The Kings' Next Match

The Kings are playing in a soccer tournament. They have learned the results of other games in the tournament, and there have been some surprises. They know that if they lose their next match, they will face a weaker team, the Pumas, in the semi-final. If they win, their opponents will be the Stars, a team with a much stronger record. Should they lose their next match on purpose?

Robyn's Swimming Rival

Robyn and Avery are rivals on the same college swimming team. They are the two best swimmers on the team. All students are required to keep a 70 percent average in their studies to be on the team. Robyn has learned that Avery is cheating by paying someone to write her assignments for her. Should Robyn tell the coach, or should she keep quiet about what she knows?

© ERPI • Reproduction prohibited

APPENDIX

Bring It All Together, B, page 133

1 You share an apartment with Jack Pierce. You know he would never hurt anyone. He is a good student who loves Northbright. He does not deserve a harsh punishment.

2 You are Suzy Lee's classmate. You have often heard her talking about carrying out acts of protest. You think she should be asked to leave the college immediately.

3 You are Jamal Jones's friend. You supported the protest. You think the college should forget about this event, as no one was seriously hurt.

4 You are Jamal Jones's classmate. You think he and his friends just want to cause trouble. They aren't serious students and should not be at Northbright.

5 You work for the Northbright campus security service. You think students have no respect for authority. They need a jail sentence to encourage other students to follow the rules.

6 You are a student counsellor at Northbright. You know that strong punishments are a waste of time. Students who get into trouble need help, not jail sentences or fines.

7 You work in the Northbright administrative building, and you watched the events on the first day. You were scared! You think these students should be given a harsh punishment.

8 You teach at Northbright. You know that the quality of student services has gotten worse. You admire the students for their actions. You don't think they should be expelled or fined.

9 You are Suzy Lee's parent. You are afraid that she will have a criminal record and that this will hurt her career prospects. She is an excellent student who wants to be a doctor.

10 You are Jack Pierce's cousin. You weren't accepted into Northbright. The college should expel these students and give their places to others who really want to study there.

11 You work for Northbright. Your job is to raise money. You know the college depends on donations from graduates. This event will hurt its reputation if the students are not expelled.

© ERPI • Reproduction prohibited

12 You are a graduate of Northbright. When you were there forty years ago, this kind of thing happened frequently. This is normal behaviour for young people.

13 You work in the finance department at Northbright. This event has cost the college a lot of money for repairs and cleaning. The students must be told to pay for these services.

14 You work in the food services department. You are thankful to the students for raising awareness of cutbacks to food services. They should be congratulated!

15 You are a good friend of George Penner. He has been away from work for medical reasons for over a year now. These students need to be punished for what they have done to him.

16 You have worked with George Penner for many years. You think he is a weak leader, and you blame him for this event. The students expressed the opinions of many other people.

17 You are a student. You have many food allergies, and the cuts to food services have made it difficult for you to eat healthily. You fully support the actions of the students.

18 You are a student. You are embarrassed to be a Northbright student. You are angry that these students have damaged the reputation of your college. They need to leave!

19 You live near the Northbright campus. You often hear students making noise. You think they need to be told that this kind of behaviour is not acceptable.

20 You have lived near Northbright for many years. You think Northbright students make an important contribution to the local community and economy. They should be supported.

21 You are a cleaner at Northbright. You had to clean up the damage to the administrative building. You would like to see these young criminals get a severe punishment.

22 You are a bus driver. You know that Northbright students rely on the local bus service. The increased cost of bus passes has hurt them. They should not be punished.

© **ERPI** • Reproduction prohibited

PHOTO CREDITS

ALAMY
p. 69, top: © Bryan Smith/ZUMA Press/Alamy.

ASSOCIATED PRESS
p.133: © AP Photo/Andy Molloy, Kennebec Journal.

GETTY IMAGES
p. 48, top: © Kyodo News; p. 48, bottom: © LLUIS GENE; p. 49, top: © Jack Guez; p. 109: © Hero Images.

DR. SALLY FOOTE
p. 117: © courtesy Dr. Sally Foote.

KHAN ACADEMY
p. 78: Khan Academy.

LUMOS
p. 49: bottom © David Lehl.

SHUTTERSTOCK
cover: © Rawpixel.com; p. 3: © Dean Drobot; p. 4, top to bottom: © Dean Drobot, © lightwavemedia, © AJR_photo, © Irina BG; p. 5, top: © Taras Verkhovynets; p. 5, bottom: © sirtravelalot; p. 11: © AndrasKiss; p. 15: © Gelner Tivadar; p. 21, top to bottom: © Bonita R. Cheshier, © dotshock, © Pavel L Photo and Video; © bbernard; p. 22, top: Brocreative; p. 22, bottom: ESB Professional; p. 23: Mitch Gunn; p. 25: © oneinchpunch; p. 26, top left to bottom right: © Ann Haritonenko, © Aleksandr Khmeliov, © El Nariz, © one_clear_vision, © Vevchic, © Anna Durinikova; p. 27, top to bottom: © Kiselev Andrey Valerevich, © Skeronov, © eyedear; p. 30: AJR_photo; p. 31: © Lucky Business; p. 34: © absolut; p. 35: © Kim Ruoff; p. 36: © Alla Iatsun; p. 37: Jose AS Reyes; p. 39: © perfectlab; p. 40, top to bottom: © Pixsooz, © Axel Bueckert, © Olaf Speier, © Filip Fuxa, © Jim Lopes, © Nestor Rizhniak; p. 41, top: © PeachLoveU; p. 41, bottom: © Roman Samokhin; p. 42: © Halfpoint; p. 45: © michaeljung; p. 51: © MikeDotta; p. 52: © Fabio Balbi; p. 53: © RossHelen; p. 54, top left to bottom right: © Enrika Samulionyte, © TaraPatta, © Gubin Yury, © valbar, © Atlaspix, © Luca Luceri; p. 55: © Ariel Celste Photography; p. 57: © Dariusz Jarzabek; p. 62, top to bottom: © meunierd, © ChameleonsEye, © Dennis van de Water, © viewfinder, © Radu Bercan; p. 66: © Happy Auer; p. 67: © Jacob Lund; p. 68, top to bottom: © Billion Photos, © aradaphotography, © Nagel Photography; p. 69, bottom: © Stockforlife; p. 71: © F8 Studio; p. 73, © DGLimages; p. 76: goodluz; p. 82, top, left to right: © O391, © Globe Turner, © Globe Turner, © Photoonlife, © Globe Turner; p. 82, bottom, left to right: © roihun matpor, © Maximumvector, © Julinzy, © Lukasz Stefanski, © charnsitr; p. 83: © Miki Studio; p. 84, top: © Jess Kraft; p. 84, bottom: © Steve Photography; p. 85, © Gaspar Janos; p. 89: © Konstantin Chagin; p. 93: © GaudiLab; p. 94: © biletskiy; p. 97, left: © HelloRF Zcool; p. 97, right: © Evan Lorne; p. 98, top left to bottom right: © Rawpixel.com, © Ugis Riba, © fuyu liu, © Arthur Palmer, © Josehp M. Arseneau, © littlenySTOCK; p. 99: © Pabkov; p. 108: © Ron Ellis; p. 112: © wavebreakmedia; p. 113, top to bottom: © Jack Frog, © AJR_photo, © Halfpoint, © Flamingo Images; p. 114, top: © StockLite; p. 114, bottom: © Mettus; p. 116: © hydebrink; p. 121: © Benny Marty; p. 122: © fotoinfot; p. 124, top to bottom: © Kate33, © Dmitri Ma, © Deyana Stefanova Robova, © Maxx-Studio; p. 126: © Snapic_Photo_Production; p. 136: © TACstock1; p. 137: © JJFarq; p. 141: © Matej Kastelic; p. 142: © michaeljung; p. 147: © Gorodenkoff; p. 148: © RazoomGame; p. 151: © Saranyu L; p. 152: © wavebreakmedia; p. 153: © Lazarin Hristov; p. 155, top: © Anton_Ivanov; p. 155, bottom: © Anton_Ivanov; p. 156, top: © Denis Makarenko; p. 156, bottom: © Feature Flash Photo Agency; p. 157: © guruXOX; p. 158: © Rawpixel.com.

© ERPI • Reproduction prohibited

RAWPIXEL

p. 1: © Roungroat.

UNIVERSITY OF MASSACHUSETTS

p. 118: © University of Massachusetts, Biology Computer Resource Center.

UNSPLASH

p. 12: © Jannes Glas; p. 24: © Hannah Grace; p.80: © Capturing the human heart; p. 96: © Andreas Brucker; p. 123: © Robert Hickerson; p. 135: © Nhu Nguyen.

VIDEO CREDITS

UNIT 2

p. 15: "Teen Soccer Play Faces a Moral Dilemma" © Canadian Broadcasting Corporation.

UNIT 4

p. 43: "Technology, This Year's Hottest Wedding Trend" © ABC News.

UNIT 6

p. 71: "Sixteen-Year-Old Dropout is CEO of Company Potentially Worth Millions" © ABC News.

UNIT 8

p. 99: "Urban Parks: Good for the City and the Environment" with permission from Nicholas School.

UNIT 10

p. 126: "Meet the Judge Who Went Viral for His Creative Punishments" © ABC News.

UNIT 12

p. 151: "Xhosa and the Black Panther Movie" © ABC News.

© **ERPI** • Reproduction prohibited

NOTES

© **ERPI** • Reproduction prohibited

NOTES

© **ERPI** • Reproduction prohibited

NOTES

© **ERPI** • Reproduction prohibited